The Perfect Stranger's Guide to Funerals and Grieving Practices

The Perfect Stranger's Guide to Funerals and Grieving Practices

A Guide to Etiquette in Other People's Religious Ceremonies

Edited by Stuart M. Matlins

Walking Together, Finding the Way

SKYLIGHT PATHS Publishing

WOODSTOCK, VERMONT

Library of Congress Cataloging-in-Publication Data
The perfect stranger's guide to funerals and grieving practices : a guide to etiquette in other people's religious ceremonies / edited by Stuart M. Matlins.
          p. cm.
ISBN 1-893361-20-9 (pbk.)
1. Religious etiquette—United States. 2. United States—Religion—20th century. I. Matlins, Stuart M.
BJ2071 .P47 2000
395.2'3—dc21
                          00-059574

10 9 8 7 6 5 4 3 2 1

Manufactured in the United States of America
Cover design by Drena Fagen
Text design by Chelsea Dippel

Published by SkyLight Paths Publishing
A Division of LongHill Partners, Inc.
Sunset Farm Offices, Route 4, P.O. Box 237
Woodstock, VT 05091
Tel: (802) 457-4000   Fax: (802) 457-4004
www.skylightpaths.com

Contents

Acknowledgments

A book such as this is the product of many contributions by many people. It could be no other way given the broad tapestry of religions in North America. This book, with its focus on etiquette at funerals and for grieving practices, is based on the two award-winning volumes of *How to Be a Perfect Stranger: A Guide to Etiquette in Other People's Religious Ceremonies*.

Instrumental in the evolution of *How to Be a Perfect Stranger* were Richard A. Siegel and William Shanken, who developed the original concept and helped get the first volume into gear. Stuart M. Matlins, publisher of SkyLight Paths, developed the methodology for obtaining the information, and with Arthur J. Magida, editorial director of SkyLight Paths, oversaw the research and writing and provided the impetus for the project. Sandra Korinchak, editor, shepherded the project from start to finish with the help of Jennifer Goneau, editorial assistant. Research assistant Susan Parks helped ensure that certain denominations responded promptly to our requests. And Jordan D. Wood generously assumed an initiative that delighted us all. Michael Schwartzentruber, series editor of Northstone Publishing, compiled the Canadian data.

The Native American/First Nations information was provided by Dan Wildcat, a member of the Wyuchi Tribe of Oklahoma and a sociology professor at the Haskell Indian Nations University in Lawrence, Kansas.

All other chapters were based on information obtained from an extensive questionnaire filled out by clergy and other religious experts coast-to-coast. Without the help of the following, this book would never have become a reality:

Timothy Addington, Executive Director of Ministry Advancement,
The Evangelical Free Church of North America, Minneapolis, Minnesota

Rev. E. Wayne Antworth, Director of Stewardship and Communications,
The Reformed Church in America, New York, New York

Dr. Satyendra Banerjee, priest and past-president,
Bengali Cultural Society of British Columbia

Leroy Beachy, Beachy Amish Mennonite, Millersburg, Ohio

Ronald R. Brannon, General Secretary,
The Wesleyan Church, Indianapolis, Indiana

Rabbi Gary M. Bretton-Granatoor, Director of Interreligious Affairs,
Union of American Hebrew Congregations (Reform),
New York, New York

Ellen K. Campbell, Executive Director,
Canadian Unitarian Council, Toronto, Ontario

Marj Carpenter, former Mission Interpreter,
Presbyterian Church (USA), Louisville, Kentucky

Sharon Glidden Cole, Administrative Assistant,
Executive Offices, The Christian and Missionary Alliance,
Colorado Springs, Colorado

Glenn Cooper, former Director of Communications,
The Presbyterian Church in Canada, Pictou, Nova Scotia

Archpriest George Corey, Vicar,
Antiochian Orthodox Archdiocese, New York, New York

Scott Dickson, Public Affairs (Canada), Jehovah's Witnesses,
Watch Tower Bible and Tract Society of Canada

Alf Dumont (member, First Nations),
St. John's United Church, Alliston, Ontario

Rev. Ora W. Eads, General Superintendent,
The Christian Congregation, Inc., LaFollette, Tennessee

Rabbi Moshe Edelman, Associate Director of Regions and
Director of Leadership Development,
United Synagogue of Conservative Judaism, New York, New York

Eugene J. Fisher, Associate Director of the Secretariat for
Ecumenical and Interreligious Affairs of the National Conference
of Catholic Bishops, Washington, D.C.

Ted George, Librarian, Greek Orthodox Cathedral of the Annunciation,
Baltimore, Maryland

Rev. Lance Gifford, Rector, St. John's Episcopal Church,
Baltimore, Maryland

James S. Golding, Editor, *The [Greek] Orthodox Observer,*
New York, New York

Steven D. Goodman, Professor of Indian and Tibetan Buddhism,
Institute of Buddhist Studies, Berkeley, California

Lois Hammond, Evangelical Free Church of Canada,
Langley, British Columbia

Father Gregory Havrilak, Director of Communications,
Orthodox Church in North America, New York, New York

Marvin Hein, General Secretary,
The General Conference of Mennonite Brethren, Fresno, California

Hoyt Hickman, now retired from the General Board of Discipleship,
United Methodist Church, Nashville, Tennessee

Rev. Donald E. Hodgins, Central Canada District,
The Wesleyan Church of Canada, Belleville, Ontario

Hans Holznagel, Public Relations Manager,
United Church of Christ, Cleveland, Ohio

Ibrahim Hooper, Council on American-Islamic Relations,
Washington, D.C.

Bede Hubbard, Assistant General Secretary,
Canadian Conference of Catholic Bishops, Ottawa, Ontario

John Hurley, Archivist and Public Relations Officer,
Unitarian Universalist Association of Congregations,
Boston, Massachusetts

Ralph Janes, Communications Director,
Seventh-day Adventist Church in Canada

Rev. B. Edgar Johnson, Former General Secretary,
The Church of the Nazarene, Kansas City, Missouri

Wesley Johnson, Executive Assistant,
The Evangelical Free Church of North America, Minneapolis, Minnesota

Hari Dharam Kaur Khalsa, The Mukhia Sardarni Sahiba,
Sikh Dharma of New Mexico, Española, New Mexico

Rev. Dr. Ralph Lebold, Past President Conrad Grebel College,
University of Waterloo, Waterloo, Ontario

Don LeFevre, Manager of Public Affairs Department,
The Church of Jesus Christ of Latter-day Saints, Salt Lake City, Utah

David A. Linscheid, Communications Director,
General Conference Mennonite Church, Newton, Kansas

Barbara Liotscos, Consultant for Ministry and Worship,
The Anglican Church of Canada, Toronto, Ontario

Stan Litke, Executive Director,
Christian Church (Disciples of Christ) in Canada, Calgary, Alberta

Dr. Gordon MacDonald, Pentecostal Holiness Church of Canada,
Surrey, British Columbia

Rev. David Mahsman, Director of News and Information,
The Lutheran Church–Missouri Synod, St. Louis, Missouri

Mike McDonald, Pulpit Minister, The Church of Christ, Monahans, Texas

The Very Reverend Protopresbyter Frank P. Miloro,
The American Carpatho-Russian Orthodox Greek Catholic
Diocese of the U.S.A., Johnstown, Pennsylvania

Mr. Ronald R. Minor, General Secretary,
The Pentecostal Church of God, Joplin, Missouri

Dana Mullen, Clerk–Representative Meeting,
Canadian Yearly Meeting, Ottawa, Ontario

Dr. Paul Nelson, Director for Worship,
Evangelical Lutheran Church in America, Chicago, Illinois

Father Louis Noplos, Assistant Pastor,
Greek Orthodox Cathedral of the Annunciation, Baltimore, Maryland

Rev. Dr. David Ocea, The Romanian Orthodox
Episcopate of North America, Grass Lake, Minnesota

Sara Palmer, Program Secretary, The Wider Quaker Fellowship,
Philadelphia, Pennsylvania

Mark Parent, Ph.D., Pereaux United Baptist Church,
Pereaux, Nova Scotia

Richard Payne, Dean, Institute of Buddhist Studies,
Berkeley, California

Wardell Payne, Research Consultant on African American
Religions, Washington, D.C.

Laurie Peach, Staff Writer,
The First Church of Christ, Scientist, Boston, Massachusetts

Pal S. Purewal, former president,
Sikh Society of Alberta, Edmonton, Alberta

Rev. Frank Reid, Senior Pastor,
Bethel African Methodist Episcopal Church, Baltimore, Maryland

Dr. George W. Reid, Director of the Biblical Research Institute,
Seventh-day Adventists, Silver Spring, Maryland

Raymond Richardson, Writing Department,
Jehovah's Witnesses, Brooklyn, New York

Rev. John Roberts, Pastor,
Woodbrook Baptist Church, Baltimore, Maryland

Michael R. Rothaar, Acting Director for Worship,
Evangelical Lutheran Church in America, Chicago, Illinois

Howard E. Royer, Director of Interpretation,
The Church of the Brethren, Elgin, Indiana

John Schlenck, Librarian and Music Director,
Vedanta Society of New York, New York

Bhante Seelawimala, Professor of Theravada Buddhism,
Institute of Buddhist Studies, Berkeley, California

Bruce Smith, Public Affairs,
The Church of Jesus Christ of Latter-day Saints, North York, Ontario

Rabbi David Sulomm Stein, Beit Tikvah Congregation
(Reconstructionist), Baltimore, Maryland

Dr. Suwanda Sugunasiri, President, Buddhist Council of Canada;
Teaching Staff and Research Associate in Buddhist Studies,
Trinity College, University of Toronto

Trish Swanson, Former Director, Office of Public Information,
Baha'is of the United States, New York, New York

Imam Michael Abdur Rashid Taylor,
Islamic Chaplaincy Services Canada, Bancroft, Ontario

James Taylor, United Church of Canada,
co-founder Wood Lake Books Inc., Okanagan Centre, British Columbia

Dr. David A. Teutsch, President,
Reconstructionist Rabbinical College, Wyncote, Pennsylvania

Juleen Turnage, Secretary of Public Relations,
Assemblies of God, Springfield, Missouri

Jerry Van Marter, Mission Interpreter and International News,
Presbyterian Church (USA), Louisville, Kentucky

Lois Volstad, Executive Secretary, Executive Offices,
The Christian and Missionary Alliance, Colorado Springs, Colorado

Rev. Kenn Ward, editor of *Canada Lutheran*, Winnipeg, Manitoba

Deborah Weiner, Director, Public Relations,
Unitarian Universalist Association of Congregations, Boston, Massachusetts

Rabbi Tzvi Hersh Weinreb, Shomrei Emunah Congregation
(Orthodox), Baltimore, Maryland

M. Victor Westberg, Manager, Committees on Publications,
The First Church of Christ, Scientist, Boston, Massachusetts

Ronald D. Williams, Communications Officer,
International Church of the Foursquare Gospel, Los Angeles, California

Clifford L. Willis, Director of News and Information,
The Christian Church (Disciples of Christ), Indianapolis, Indiana

Pamela Zivari, Director, Office of Public Information,
Baha'is of the United States, New York, New York

Introduction

Grieving the loss of a friend, loved one, or colleague is an important process—that can be made unnecessarily awkward if you're unfamiliar with the religious tradition in which the grieving takes place and end up uncertain about how to behave. It is no longer uncommon to be called upon to offer condolences upon the loss of a relative, friend, or colleague whose faith practices are unfamiliar to us. This can lead to an awkward situation if we are unprepared—and few people ever are really prepared for such events. Nevertheless, such exposure to the religious ways of others can give us a deep appreciation for the extraordinary diversity of faith and the variety of ways it surfaces.

Yet, we may be uncomfortable or uncertain: What do I do? Or wear? Or say? What should I *avoid* doing, wearing, saying? What will happen during the ceremony? How long will it last? What does each ritual mean? What are the basic beliefs of this particular religion?

These are just some of the practical questions that arise because of the fundamental foreignness of the experience. *The Perfect Stranger's Guide to Funerals and Grieving Practices* addresses these concerns in a straightforward and nonjudgmental manner. Its goal is to make a well-meaning guest feel comfortable, participate to the fullest extent feasible, and avoid violating anyone's religious principles. It is not intended to be a comprehensive primer on theology. It's a guidebook to a land where we may be strangers, but where, on the whole, those whose mourning we share will want us to be as comfortable, relaxed and unperturbed as possible. There is nothing more indicative of friendship than to welcome "the stranger"—and for "the stranger" to do his or her homework before entering an unfamiliar house of worship or religious ceremony.

We've all been strangers at one time or another or in one place or another. If this book helps turn the "strange" into the less "exotic" and into the less confusing (but not into the ordinary), then it will have satisfied

13

its goal of minimizing our anxiety and our confusion when face-to-face with another faith—while, at the same time, deepening our appreciation and our understanding of that faith. While we pray and worship in thousands of churches, synagogues, mosques and temples around the country, these denominational fences are not insurmountable. Indeed, these fences come complete with gates. It is often up to us find the key to those gates. We hope that this book helps in the search for that key.

A few notes on the way in which *The Perfect Stranger's Guide to Funerals and Grieving Practices* was compiled and structured:

Each chapter is devoted to a particular religion or denomination. Basic research was conducted through an extensive questionnaire that was completed in almost all cases by the national office of each religion and denomination. For those denominations whose national office did not respond to the questionnaire, we obtained responses from clergy of that particular faith. To minimize error in nuance, drafts of the entry for each chapter were forwarded for comments to those who had filled out the questionnaire.

The Perfect Stranger's Guide to Funerals and Grieving Practices is not intended as a substitute for the social common sense that should prevail at social or religious events. For example, if a chapter advises readers that guests may use a flash or a video camera, the equipment should not be used in such a way that it disrupts the religious ceremony or disturbs participants in the ceremony or other guests.

The guidelines in this book are just that. They should not be mistaken for firm and unbendable rules. Religious customs, traditions and rituals for funerals and mourning are strongly influenced by where people live and the part of the world from which their ancestors originated. As a result, there may be a variety of practices within a single denomination. This book is a general guide to funerals and mourning, and it's important to remember that *particulars* may sometimes vary broadly within individual denominations.

Terms within each chapter are those used by that religion. For example, the terms "New Testament" and "Old Testament" appear in several chapters about various Christian denominations. Some Jewish people may find this disconcerting since they recognize only one testament. The purpose is not to offend, but to portray these religions as they portray themselves. The goal of this book, one must remember, is to enable us to be "a perfect stranger." And "perfection" might well begin with recognizing that when we join others in participating in events in their religion's vernacular, we are obliged, as guests, to know the customs, rituals and language of the event.

For future editions of *The Perfect Stranger's Guide to Funerals and Grieving Practices*, we encourage readers to write to us and suggest ways in which this book could be made more useful to them and to others. Are there additional subjects that future editions should cover? Have important subtleties been missed? We see this book—and the evolution of our unique North American society—as an ongoing work-in-progress, and we welcome your comments. Please write to:

Editors, *The Perfect Stranger's Guide to Funerals and Grieving Practices*
SkyLight Paths Publishing
Sunset Farm Offices, Rte. 4
P.O. Box 237
Woodstock, Vermont 05091

1

African American Methodist Churches

(known as the African Methodist Episcopal Church; the African Methodist Episcopal Zion Church; the Christian Methodist Episcopal Church; the Union American Methodist Episcopal Church, Inc.; and the African Union First Colored Methodist Protestant Church)

HISTORY AND BELIEFS

The African American Methodist churches began in the late 18th century and throughout the 19th century as a reaction to racial discrimination. The broader Methodist Church had originated in the early 18th century in England under the preaching of John Wesley, an Anglican priest who was a prodigious evangelical preacher, writer and organizer. While a student at Oxford University, he and his brother had led the Holy Club of devout students, whom scoffers called the "Methodists."

Wesley's teachings affirmed the freedom of human will as promoted by grace. He saw each person's depth of sin matched by the height of sanctification to which the Holy Spirit, the empowering spirit of God, can lead persons of faith.

Although Wesley remained an Anglican and disavowed attempts to form a new church, Methodism eventually became another church body. During a conference in Baltimore, Maryland, in 1784, the Methodist Church was founded as an ecclesiastical organization and the first Methodist bishop in the United States was elected.

Blacks had originally been attracted to the Methodist Church because its original evangelism made no distinctions between the races, and John

17

Wesley, the founder of Methodism, had strongly denounced slavery and the African slave trade on the grounds that they were contrary to the will of God. Initially, many Methodists—clergy and laity—opposed slavery, called upon church members to desist from trafficking in slaves, and urged them to free any slaves they did own. But as Methodists became more numerous in the South, the Church gradually muted its opposition to slavery.

In 1787, black members of Philadelphia's St. George's Methodist Episcopal Church withdrew from the church after experiencing discrimination, and the African Methodist Episcopal Church was officially established as a denomination on April 16, 1816.

The African Methodist Episcopal Zion Church was founded in 1796 after blacks were denied the sacraments and full participation in the John Street Methodist Church in New York City, located in a state with the largest slave population outside of the South.

And the Christian Methodist Episcopal Church was founded in 1870, four years after African American members of the Methodist Episcopal Church, South (M.E.C.S.) petitioned the Church to be allowed to create a separate Church that would be governed by the M.E.C.S. In 1870, the General Conference of the M.E.C.S. voted to let black members be constituted as an independent church, not as a subordinate body. This reflected the post-Civil War period's imperatives calling for independence for African Americans and the reconstruction of American society.

Two smaller African American Methodist churches are the Union American Methodist Episcopal Church, Inc., with 15,000 members in 55 congregations, and the African Union First Colored Methodist Protestant Church, with 5,000 members in 33 congregations. Both of these were founded in 1865.

Local African American Methodist churches are called "charges." Their ministers are appointed by the bishop at an annual conference, and each church elects its own administrative board, which initiates planning and sets local goals and policies.

Number of U.S. churches:

African Methodist Episcopal: 8,000
African Methodist Episcopal Zion: 3,100
African Union First Colored Methodist Protestant Church: 33
Christian Methodist Episcopal Church: 2,300
Union American Methodist Episcopal Church, Inc.: 55

Number of U. S. members:
African Methodist Episcopal: 3.5 million
African Methodist Episcopal Zion: 1.2 million
African Union First Colored Methodist Protestant Church: 5,000
Christian Methodist Episcopal Church: 718,900
Union American Methodist Episcopal Church, Inc.: 15,000
(*data from the* Directory of American Religious Bodies *and the*
1998 Yearbook of American and Canadian Churches)

FUNERALS AND MOURNING

African American Methodist denominations affirm that life is eternal and that, in faith, one can look forward to life with God after death.

African American Methodists have diverse beliefs about afterlife and are generally content to look forward to it as a glorious mystery. Funerals have as their purposes: 1) expressing grief and comforting one another in our bereavement; 2) celebrating the life of the deceased; and 3) affirming faith in life with God after death. Which of these is most emphasized at the funeral depends on the circumstances of the death and the extent of the faith of the deceased.

BEFORE THE CEREMONY

How soon after the death does the funeral usually take place?
Usually within two to three days.

What should one who is not a member of an African American Methodist denomination do upon hearing of the death of a member of that faith?
Telephone or visit the bereaved.

APPROPRIATE ATTIRE

Men: A jacket and tie. No head covering is required.

Women: A dress. Open-toed shoes and modest jewelry are permissible. No head covering is required.

There are no rules regarding colors of clothing, but somber, dark colors are recommended for men and women.

GIFTS

Is it appropriate to send flowers or make a contribution?

Yes. Send flowers to the home of the bereaved. Contributions are also optional. The recommended charity may be mentioned in the deceased's obituary.

Is it appropriate to send food?

Yes. Send it to the home of the bereaved.

THE CEREMONY

Where will the ceremony take place?

At a church or funeral home.

When should guests arrive and where should they sit?

Arrive early. Ushers will advise them where to sit.

If arriving late, are there times when a guest should *not* enter the ceremony?

No.

Will the bereaved family be present at the church or funeral home before the ceremony?

Possibly.

Is there a traditional greeting for the family?

Simply express your condolences.

Will there be an open casket?

Usually.

Is a guest expected to view the body?

This is entirely optional.

What is appropriate behavior upon viewing the body?

Silent prayer.

Who are the major officiants at the ceremony and what do they do?

■ *A pastor,* who officiates.

To indicate the order of the ceremony:

A program will be provided.

Will a guest who is not a member of an African American Methodist denomination be expected to do anything other than sit?

No.

Are there any parts of the ceremony in which a guest who is not a member of an African American Methodist denomination should *not* participate?

No.

If not disruptive to the ceremony, is it okay to:

▪ **Take pictures?** No.
▪ **Use a video camera?** No.
▪ **Use a flash camera?** No.
▪ **Use a tape recorder?** No.

Will contributions to the church be collected at the ceremony?

No.

THE INTERMENT

Should guests attend the interment?

Yes.

Whom should one ask for directions?

The funeral director.

What happens at the graveside?

Prayers are recited by the pastor and the body is committed to the ground. If there has been a cremation, which is done privately before the service, the ashes are either buried or put in a vault.

Do guests who are not members of an African American Methodist denomination participate at the graveside ceremony?

No. They are simply present.

COMFORTING THE BEREAVED

Is it appropriate to visit the home of the bereaved after the funeral?

Yes, at any mutually convenient time. How long one stays depends on your closeness to the bereaved. Typically, one stays about 30 to 45 minutes.

Will there be a religious service at home of the bereaved?

No.

Will food be served?

No.

How soon after the funeral will a mourner usually return to a normal work schedule?

This is entirely at the discretion of the bereaved.

How soon after the funeral will a mourner usually return to a normal social schedule?

This is entirely at the discretion of the bereaved.

Are there mourning customs to which a friend who is not a member of an African American Methodist denomination should be sensitive?

No.

Are there rituals for observing the anniversary of the death?

There may be a service commemorating the deceased.

2

Assemblies of God

HISTORY AND BELIEFS

In 1914, when the Assemblies of God were formed, America had, for several years, been in the midst of a major revival movement. Many involved spontaneously spoke "in tongues" (or in a language unknown to those speaking it) and claims were made of divine healing that saved lives. Since many of these experiences were associated with the coming of the Holy Spirit (the empowering quality of God) on the Day of Pentecost, participants in the revival were called Pentecostals.

After mainline churches divorced themselves from the revival phenomenon, about 300 Pentecostal leaders met in Hot Springs, Arkansas. After three days of prayer, they decided to organize themselves not as a new denomination, but as a loose-knit fellowship called the General Council of the Assemblies of God. Two years later, the Council realized the need to establish standards of doctrinal truths.

In part, this Statement of Fundamental Truths asserts that the Bible is divinely inspired and is infallible; the one true God created earth and heaven, redeems humanity from its sins and consists of the Father, the Son (Jesus Christ) and the Holy Spirit; Jesus has always existed and is without beginning or end; humanity was created good and upright, but, by falling into sin, incurred physical and spiritual death; humanity's only hope for salvation from sin and spiritual death is through Christ.

The Assemblies of God is one of the more quickly growing churches in the United States: Since 1960, membership has grown from around 500,000 to more than 1.4 million. The Church is especially keen on using conversion to swell its ranks. In the last decade, the largest number of conversions—61,272—has been in the Church's southwest region (California, Nevada, Arizona and Colorado). Many of these new members are Hispanic-speaking.

U.S. churches: 12,000
U.S. membership: 1.4 million
(1998 data from the Assemblies of God)

FUNERALS AND MOURNING

Members of the Assemblies of God believe that all Christians who have died will one day rise from their graves and meet the Lord in the air. Meanwhile, Christians who are still alive will be raptured (or caught up with those who have risen from their graves) and will also be with the Lord. All who have thus joined with God will live forever.

An Assemblies of God funeral usually begins with singing, Scripture reading or prayer. This is followed with hymns, prayer and worship to God, and a sermon by the pastor.

A ceremony in itself, the funeral service lasts about 30 to 60 minutes.

BEFORE THE CEREMONY

How soon after the death does the funeral usually take place?
Usually, within two to three days; sometimes, within one week.

What should someone who is not a member of the Assemblies of God do upon hearing of the death of a member of that faith?
Telephone or visit the bereaved to offer condolences and sympathies and offer to assist in any way possible.

APPROPRIATE ATTIRE

Men: A jacket and tie. No head covering is required.

Women: A dress or a skirt and blouse. Clothing need not cover the arms and hems need not reach below the knees. Open-toed shoes and modest jewelry are permissible. No head covering is required.

Dark, somber colors for clothing are advised.

GIFTS

Is it appropriate to send flowers or make a contribution?
Flowers may be sent to the funeral home or church where the funeral service is held. Contributions may be sent to the home of the bereaved after the funeral.

Is it appropriate to send food?
Yes.

THE CEREMONY

Where will the ceremony take place?
Either in a church or a funeral home.

When should guests arrive and where should they sit?
Arrive at the time for which the service has been scheduled. Ushers usually advise guests where to sit.

If arriving late, are there times when a guest should *not* enter the ceremony?
No.

Will the bereaved family be present at the church or funeral home before the ceremony?
Not usually.

Is there a traditional greeting for the family?
Just offer your condolences.

Will there be an open casket?
Usually.

Is a guest expected to view the body?
This is optional.

What is appropriate behavior upon viewing the body?
Walk past the casket, then take a seat in the church sanctuary or the room in the funeral parlor where the service will be held.

Who are the major officiants at the ceremony and what do they do?
- *The pastor*, who delivers a brief sermon and tribute to the deceased.
- *Musicians*, who sing one or two songs.

What books are used?

The Old and New Testaments. Most commonly used is the New International Version of the King James translation of the Bible, which is released by several publishers.

To indicate the order of the ceremony:

A program will be distributed.

Will a guest who is not a member of the Assemblies of God be expected to do anything other than sit?

Guests of other faiths are expected to stand when other guests rise during the service. It is optional for them to kneel and to sing with the congregants and to join them in reading prayers aloud.

Are there any parts of the ceremony in which a guest who is not a member of the Assemblies of God should *not* participate?

No.

If not disruptive to the ceremony, is it okay to:
◘ **Take pictures?** Possibly.
◘ **Use a flash?** Possibly.
◘ **Use a video camera?** Possibly.
◘ **Use a tape recorder?** Possibly.

(Note: Policies regarding still and video cameras and tape recorders vary with each church. Check with the local pastor before using such equipment during a service.)

Will contributions to the church be collected at the ceremony?

No.

THE INTERMENT

Should guests attend the interment?

Attendance is optional.

Whom should one ask for directions?

An usher or the funeral director.

What happens at the graveside?

There are prayers, songs and Scripture readings.

Do guests who are not members of the Assemblies of God participate at the graveside ceremony?

No, they are simply present.

COMFORTING THE BEREAVED

Is it appropriate to visit the home of the bereaved after the funeral?
Yes, if one knows the family well.

Will there be a religious service at the home of the bereaved?
No.

Will food be served?
Possibly.

How soon after the funeral will a mourner usually return to a normal work schedule?
A week or two, depending upon individual preference. The Church has no set tradition.

How soon after the funeral will a mourner usually return to a normal social schedule?
This is entirely the choice of the bereaved, since the Church has no set tradition. It may be one or two weeks, or more, and is often primarily determined by local cultural traditions.

Are there mourning customs to which a friend who is not a member of the Assemblies of God should be sensitive?
No.

Are there rituals for observing the anniversary of the death?
No.

3

Baha'i

HISTORY AND BELIEFS

The Baha'i religion sprang out of an Islamic movement known as the Babi faith, which was founded in the mid-19th century in Persia (now southern Iran) by Mirza Ali Muhammad, a direct descendent of the Prophet Muhammad. By proclaiming himself to be the Bab, which literally means "gate" or "door," Ali Muhammad announced that he was the forerunner of the Universal Messenger of God, who would usher in an era of justice and peace.

In 1850, the Bab was killed by a firing squad in Tabriz, Persia, upon the order of the grand vizier of the new Shah of Iran. The grand vizier was acting on behalf of traditional Islamic clergy in his country, who were alarmed at what they perceived to be the heretical doctrine being taught by the Bab and also by the fact that he was gaining followers.

In 1863, one of the Bab's 18 original closest disciples, Baha'u'llah, declared, while he was in exile in Iraq, that he was "He Whom God Shall Manifest," the messianic figure whom the Bab had predicted. He was soon banished by the Iraqi government to Istanbul and then to Adrianapole, where he stayed for five years.

Agitation from opponents caused the Turkish government to send the exiles to Acre, Palestine, where Baha'u'llah spent his last years. Upon his death, his eldest son, Abdu'l-Baha, "The Servant of Baha," led the faith, as had been determined in his father's will. With his death in 1921, leadership fell, as stipulated in Abdu'l-Baha's will, to his eldest grandson, Shoghi Effendi, "The Guardian of the Cause of God," who devoted himself to expanding the worldwide Baha'i community, establishing its central administrative offices in Haifa, and translating the writings of his great-grandfather, Baha'u'llah.

Central to Baha'i beliefs is the unity of all religions and of all humanity. God, Baha'is teach, may be unknowable, but the divine presence manifests itself in various ways. Among these are the creation of the world and the prophets, beginning with Adam, and continuing through the Jewish prophets, Buddha, Krishna, Zoroaster, Jesus and Muhammad, who was succeeded by Baha'u'llah. Each prophet represents a divine message which was appropriate for the era in which he appeared. Baha'is believe that other prophets may come in the future, and that there is no last revelation or final prophet.

Members are elected to Baha'i's approximately 20,000 local spiritual councils, of which there are about 1,700 in the United States, and 324 in Canada. Members are also elected to 174 national spiritual assemblies throughout the world. These culminate in a Universal House of Justice, which has administrative, judicial and legislative functions and the authority to frame new rules for situations not provided for in the writings of Baha'u'llah.

There are now more than five million Baha'is in 233 countries and territories. Throughout the world, the Baha'i faith has only seven houses of worship, one on each continent. The house of worship in North America is in Wilmette, Illinois. Locally, Baha'is may meet for worship or for communal activities in homes or Baha'i centers. The minimum number of Baha'is that can comprise a local community is two, but nine are required for a local spiritual council.

U.S. communities: 7,000
U.S. membership: 130,000
(data from the Office of Public Information, Baha'is of the United States)

Canadian communities: 1,400
Canadian membership: 29,000
(data from the Office of Public Affairs, Baha'is of Canada)

FUNERALS AND MOURNING

The Baha'i faith teaches that there is a separate, rational soul for every human. It provides the underlying animation for the body and is our real self. Upon the death of the body, the soul is freed from its ties with the physical body and the surrounding physical world, and begins its journey through the spiritual world. Baha'is understand the spiritual world to be a timeless, placeless extension of our own universe, and not a physically remote or removed place.

Heaven is envisioned partly as a state of nearness to God; hell is a state of remoteness from God. Each state is a natural consequence of the efforts of an individual—or the lack of them—to develop spiritually. The key to spiritual progress is to follow the path outlined by the various Prophets of God, who include Adam, Moses, Buddha, Krishna, Zoroaster, Jesus and Muhammad, and Baha'u'llah.

Beyond this, the exact nature of afterlife remains a mystery.

While the Baha'i faith is relatively free of teachings regarding the actual rituals of funerals, it does advise that the deceased should not be embalmed, unless it is required by state law. Also the deceased should be buried within one hour's travel time from the place of death since the Baha'i faith teaches that we are all world citizens and should not be attached to any particular geographic site.

BEFORE THE CEREMONY

How soon after the death does the funeral usually take place?

Usually within two or three days.

What should a non-Baha'i do upon hearing of the death of a member of that faith?

Convey your condolences to the bereaved either by telephone or a visit to their home.

APPROPRIATE ATTIRE

Men: Personal preference for attire, and one's own sense of reverence, are the only criteria. This may range from jacket and tie to slacks or jeans. No head covering is required.

Women: Personal preference for attire, and one's own sense of reverence, are the only criteria. This may range from a dress or skirt to slacks or jeans. Clothing need not cover the arms or reach below the knees. No head covering is required. Women may wear open-toed shoes and/or modest jewelry.

There are no rules regarding colors of clothing, but these should conform to social and cultural custom.

GIFTS

Is it appropriate to send flowers or make a contribution?

Yes. Flowers may be sent either to the home of the bereaved before or after the funeral or to the funeral itself. Contributions may be made to a fund or charity designated by the bereaved or before death by the deceased, but non-Baha'is cannot contribute to a Baha'i fund.

Is it appropriate to send food?

Food may be sent to the home of the bereaved before or after the funeral. No specific types of food are best to send or are prohibited.

THE CEREMONY

Where will the ceremony take place?

At the local house of worship or at a funeral home.

When should guests arrive and where should they sit?

Arrive early or at the time for which the service has been called. Ushers may be available to advise guests on where to sit.

If arriving late, are there times when a guest should *not* enter the ceremony?

No.

Will the bereaved family be present before the ceremony?

Possibly.

Is there a traditional greeting for the family?

No. Simply express your condolences.

Will there be an open casket?

Rarely, since the Baha'i faith does not allow embalming.

Is a guest expected to view the body?

This is entirely optional.

What is appropriate behavior upon viewing the body?

The Baha'i faith does not ordain certain behavior at such moments since open caskets are so rare.

Who are the major officiants at the ceremony and what do they do?

Whoever the family asks to officiate. They will see that the service is carried out according to the family's wishes.

What books are used?

A prayer book, which is usually *Baha'i Prayers* (Wilmette, Ill.: National Spiritual Assemblies of the Baha'is of the United States, 1991). This is a selection of writings by Baha'u'llah, Abdu'l Baha, and Shoghi Effendi. Readings from sacred Baha'i writings are often taken from *The Gleanings* by Baha'u'llah (Wilmette, Ill.: Baha'i Publishing Trust, 1976). Other religious writings, prose or poetry may be also be read.

To indicate the order of the ceremony:

There may be periodic announcements or a program may be distributed.

Will a guest who is not a Baha'i be expected to do anything other than sit?

No.

Are there any parts of the ceremony in which a guest who is not a Baha'i should *not* participate?

No.

If not disruptive to the ceremony, is it okay to:

▪ **Take pictures?** Possibly, depending on the preference of the family members.

▪ **Use a flash?** Possibly, depending on the preference of the family members.

▪ **Use a video camera?** Possibly, depending on the preference of the family members.

▪ **Use a tape recorder?** Possibly, depending on the preference of the family members.

Will contributions to the house of worship be collected at the ceremony?

No.

THE INTERMENT

Should guests attend the interment?

Yes.

Whom should one ask for directions?

Family members or the funeral director.

What happens at the graveside?

A particular Baha'i prayer for the deceased may be recited at the graveside.

Do guests who are not Baha'is participate at the graveside ceremony?

Depending on a guest's relationship with the deceased, the bereaved family may possibly ask a guest to read aloud some prayers to those gathered at the funeral.

COMFORTING THE BEREAVED

Is it appropriate to visit the home of the bereaved after the funeral?

Yes. The timing of the visit entirely depends on the personal preference of the visitor and the bereaved.

Will there be a religious service at the home of the bereaved?

No.

Will food be served?

Probably.

How soon after the funeral will a mourner usually return to a normal work schedule?

The Baha'i faith ordains no particular mourning period. The length of a mourner's absence from work depends entirely on the individual mourner.

How soon after the funeral will a mourner usually return to a normal social schedule?

The Baha'i faith ordains no particular mourning period. The length of a mourner's absence from social events depends entirely on the individual mourner.

Are there mourning customs to which a friend who is not a Baha'i should be sensitive?

No, since the Baha'i faith ordains no particular mourning customs.

Are there rituals for observing the anniversary of the death?

No.

4

Baptist

HISTORY AND BELIEFS

The Baptist churches descend from the spiritual ferment generated by 17th century English Puritanism. Essentially, Baptists believe in the authority of the Bible, the right to privately interpret it, baptizing only those old enough to profess belief for themselves and strict separation of church and state.

Although there are about two dozen different branches and divisions of Baptist churches in the United States, there are essentially two separate schools of the faith: The General and the Particular. General Baptists believe in a universal atonement in which Christ died for all; Particular Baptists believe in the limited or "particular" death of Christ for believers only.

The movement began in England in the early 17th century. Its founder, John Smyth, moved to Holland in 1607 seeking religious liberty. Some early founders of Massachusetts, including the first president of Harvard, held Baptist beliefs. Although the first Baptist church in the colonies was founded in Providence, Rhode Island, in 1639, Philadelphia became the center of Baptist life during the colonial era.

In 1845, the white Baptist churches had separated into a northern and a southern group, with the northern division opposed to the extension of slavery. After the Civil War, the number of Black churches increased swiftly, mostly because Baptist principles appealed to Blacks and also because the autonomy allowed in individual churches meant that Black Baptist churches could operate without interference from white society. Canadian Baptists did not suffer from racial disunity but from theological disunity arising out of the Fundamentalist-Modernist controversy of the 1920s.

Today, the two largest Baptist denominations are the Southern Baptist Convention and the National Baptist Convention, U.S.A. Inc. The former has more than 15 million members and its founding in 1845 centered around a missionary impulse. The latter, with about eight million members, is the largest African-American religious association in the United States.

In Canada, three Baptist groups are significant: The Federation Baptists, divided into four conventions; The Fellowship Baptists; and the North American Baptists (German descent).

U.S. churches: 91,000
U.S. membership: 34 million
(data from the 1998 Yearbook of American and Canadian Churches*)*

Canadian churches: 3,137
Canadian membership: 363,251
(data from the 1998 Yearbook of American and Canadian Churches*)*

FUNERALS AND MOURNING

There are two schools of belief in the Baptist faith about afterlife. One maintains that one enters Paradise immediately after death. This is based on Jesus' words on the cross to the Penitent Thief, "This day shalt be with Me in Paradise" (Luke 23:43). The other school maintains that upon Jesus' Second Coming, a trumpet will sound and the dead will be raised to Paradise. This is based on Paul's writings in First Corinthians (15:32). The funeral service, which is a ceremony in itself, lasts about 30 to 60 minutes.

BEFORE THE CEREMONY

How soon after the death does the funeral usually take place?
Within one week.

What should a non-Baptist do upon hearing of the death of a member of that faith?
Telephone or visit the bereaved to offer condolences and sympathies.

APPROPRIATE ATTIRE

Men: A suit or a sport jacket and tie. No head covering is required.

Women: A dress. Clothing should cover the arms and hems should reach below the knees. Open-toed shoes and modest jewelry are allowed. No head covering is required.

Dark, somber colors are advised.

GIFTS

Is it appropriate to send flowers or make a contribution?

Flowers may be sent to the home of the bereaved before the funeral or to the church or funeral home where the funeral will take place. Contributions to a particular charity may be sent to the home of the bereaved before or after the funeral. The amount of the contribution is at the discretion of the donor. Such gifts should be presented to the spouse or adult children of the deceased.

Is it appropriate to send food?

Food may be sent to the home of the bereaved after the funeral.

THE CEREMONY

Where will the ceremony take place?

Either in a church or a funeral home.

When should guests arrive and where should they sit?

Arrive about 10 minutes before the time for which the ceremony has been called. Ushers will advise guests where to sit.

If arriving late, are there times when a guest should *not* enter the ceremony?

Do not enter when the bereaved family is entering or during prayers.

Will the bereaved family be present at the church or funeral home before the ceremony?

No.

Is there a traditional greeting for the family?

No. Just offer your condolences.

Will there be an open casket?

Usually.

Is a guest expected to view the body?

This is optional.

What is appropriate behavior upon viewing the body?

Join the line of viewers and view the body silently and somberly.

Who are the major officiants at the ceremony and what do they do?

▪ *The pastor*, who performs the service.

▪ *Musicians*, who provide music before, during and after the service.

What books are used?

Several translations of the Bible may be used, especially the King James Version, the New International Version, and the New Revised Standard Version. All are distributed by several publishers.

To indicate the order of the ceremony:

A program or bulletin will be distributed.

Will a guest who is not a Baptist be expected to do anything other than sit?

Guests of other faiths are expected to stand, kneel, read prayers aloud and sing with those present, unless this violates their religious beliefs. If one chooses not to kneel or stand, remain seated.

Are there any parts of the ceremony in which a guest who is not a Baptist should *not* participate?

No, although, very rarely, communion (or the Lord's Supper) is offered at funeral ceremonies. In some churches, communion is offered only to members of that congregation. In such cases, follow the cues of those present, ask a fellow guest for guidance or ask a pastor for advice before the service begins.

If not disruptive to the ceremony, is it okay to:

▪ **Take pictures?** No.

▪ **Use a flash?** No.

▪ **Use a video camera?** No.

▪ **Use a tape recorder?** No.

Will contributions to the church be collected at the ceremony?

No.

THE INTERMENT

Should guests attend the interment?

Yes.

Whom should one ask for directions?

Either ask the funeral director or follow the funeral procession to the cemetery.

What happens at the graveside?

During a brief service, Scriptures are read, prayers are recited and the casket is committed to the ground.

Do guests who are not Baptists participate at the graveside ceremony?

No. They are simply present.

COMFORTING THE BEREAVED

Is it appropriate to visit the home of the bereaved after the funeral?

Yes. It is appropriate to do so after the burial. During such visits, happy times during the life of the deceased are recalled and spoken about. A visit of no more than 30 minutes is fitting.

Will there be a religious service at the home of the bereaved?

No.

Will food be served?

Yes, but no alcoholic beverages. It would be considered impolite for a visitor not to eat. No grace or benediction will be recited before or after eating or drinking.

How soon after the funeral will a mourner usually return to a normal work schedule?

Possibly in one week, although there are no doctrinal prescriptions.

How soon after the funeral will a mourner usually return to a normal social schedule?

Possibly two months, although there are no doctrinal prescriptions.

Are there mourning customs to which a friend who is not a Baptist should be sensitive?

No.

Are there rituals for observing the anniversary of the death?

There is usually no formal remembrance in a church, but there are often quiet commemorations of the death within the family of the deceased.

5

Buddhist

HISTORY AND BELIEFS

Buddhism was founded in the sixth century B.C. in northern India by Siddhartha Gautama, who was born as the son to a king in what is now southern Nepal. Warned by a sage that his son would become either an ascetic or a universal monarch, the king confined his son to home. A few years after marrying and having a child of his own, Siddhartha escaped from his father's palace around the age of 29. Since he had been sheltered for his entire life from the pains of life, he was shocked when he beheld three men. The first was old and weak; the second was ill and diseased; the last was dead. Each represented different aspects of the impermanence inherent in all forms of earthly existence. He also saw a religious ascetic, who represented the possibility of a solution to these frailties.

Wandering in search of peace, Siddhartha tried many disciplines, including severe asceticism, until he came to the Bodhi Tree (the Tree of Enlightenment). He sat there in meditation until, at the age of 35, he became a Buddha, or one who is enlightened.

In his first sermon after achieving enlightenment, the Buddha spoke of the Four Noble Truths and the Noble Eightfold Path. These succinctly comprise the Buddha's insights into the essential ways of life and how to achieve spiritual liberation. The Buddha died at the age of 80. His last words were for his disciples not to depend on him, but on the *dharma*, or Buddhist teachings.

In subsequent centuries, Buddhism flowered in Asia. Asian immigrants to the United States from the early third of the 19th century to the present have brought Buddhism to America. The first significant influence of

Buddhist values and ideas on American intellectuals seems to have occurred in the 1830s in the writings of the New England transcendentalists. More recently, Buddhism has appealed to members of the Beat culture of the 1950s, the counterculture of the 1960s and the subsequent New Age movement.

In Canada, Buddhism may have arrived as early as the middle of the 19th century when the Chinese arrived, first from California and then from Hong Kong. World Buddhism (i.e., the many cultural Buddhisms from all over the world) began to impact on Canada only after the Canadian multiculturalism policy of the late 1960s. The three major Buddhist centers are Toronto, Vancouver and Montreal.

U. S. temples: Not available
U.S. membership: 500,000
(data from the 1993 Information Please Almanac*)*

Canadian temples: Not available
Canadian membership: 165,000+
(data from Stats Can, *1991)*

FUNERALS AND MOURNING

According to Buddhist belief, each individual passes through many reincarnations until they are liberated from worldly illusions and passions. They have then entered *nirvana*, Sanskrit for "a blowing out as of a flame." One enters a new incarnation immediately after death. Although the resulting being is not fully realized for nine months, a new incarnation can be interpreted as entering the womb of a woman.

Three components of any Buddhist funeral ceremony are sharing; the practice of good conduct; and developing a calm mind, or meditation.

A funeral ceremony in several Japanese Buddhist traditions consists of a eulogy with prayers at a funeral home, resembling similar ceremonies in the west. It may last one hour and 15 minutes. Cambodian, Thai and Ceylonese traditions may have up to three ceremonies, each lasting about 45 minutes. (See below for details on these ceremonies.)

BEFORE THE CEREMONY

How soon after the death does the funeral usually take place?
This varies, depending on the specific Buddhist tradition of the bereaved. In certain Japanese traditions, the funeral is usually within one week. In the Buddhist traditions of Cambodia, Ceylon and Thailand, there are three

ceremonies. In the first, which is held within two days after death, monks hold a ceremony at the home of the bereaved. In the second, which is held within two to five days after death, monks conduct a service at a funeral home. In the third, which is held seven days after the burial or cremation, monks lead a ceremony either at the home of the bereaved or at a temple. This last ceremony, called a "merit transference," seeks to generate good energy for the deceased in his or her new incarnation.

What should a non-Buddhist do upon hearing of the death of a member of that faith?
It is usually not considered appropriate to communicate with the bereaved before the funeral.

APPROPRIATE ATTIRE

Men: Standards for attire vary widely. A minority of temples expect men to wear a jacket and tie; the vast majority allow more casual dress. Loose, comfortable, casual clothing is especially recommended for those temples in which members and guests sit on meditation cushions on the floor. (Guests are advised to call the temple prior to the service for details on seating.) No head covering is required in any Buddhist temple.

Women: A minority of temples expect a dress or a skirt and blouse. The vast majority allow more casual attire. Loose, comfortable, casual clothing is especially recommended for those temples in which members and guests sit on meditation cushions on the floor. (Guests are advised to call the temple prior to the service for details on seating.) Open-toed shoes and modest jewelry are permissible. No head covering is required in any Buddhist temple.

In Japanese Buddhist traditions, dark, somber colors for clothing are advised. In Cambodian, Thai or Ceylonese traditions, white colors are advised.

GIFTS

Is it appropriate to send flowers or make a contribution?
It is appropriate to send flowers to the funeral or to make a donation of $5 to $100, depending on one's relation to the deceased. Typically, the bereaved family recommends a specific charity or cause as the recipient of donations.

Is it appropriate to send food?
No.

THE CEREMONY

Where will the ceremony take place?

In certain Japanese traditions, the ceremony is usually held at a funeral home. In Cambodian, Thai and Ceylonese traditions, the first ceremony is at the home of the bereaved, the second is at a funeral home and the third is either at the home of the bereaved or at a temple.

When should guests arrive and where should they sit?

Arrive at the time for which the service has been called. Sit wherever you wish. If the ceremony is in a funeral home, there will be pews for sitting. If held at the home or the temple of an adherent of the Cambodian, Thai or Ceylonese traditions, sitting will probably be on the floor on meditation cushions.

If arriving late, are there times when a guest should *not* enter the ceremony?

No.

Will the bereaved family be present at the temple or funeral home before the ceremony?

Yes.

Is there a traditional greeting for the family?

Just offer your condolences.

Will there be an open casket?

Always.

Is a guest expected to view the body?

Yes, because Buddhism deems viewing the body to be a valuable reminder of the impermanence of life.

What is appropriate behavior upon viewing the body?

Bow slightly toward the body as a sign of appreciation of its lesson regarding impermanence.

Who are the major officiants at the ceremony and what do they do?

- *A minister or priest*, who officiates in the Japanese tradition.
- *A monk*, who officiates in the Cambodian, Thai and Ceylonese traditions.

What books are used?

All Buddhist traditions and sects quote from the Sutras, which are the collected sayings of the Buddha.

To indicate the order of the ceremony:
Announcements may be made by the priest or monk.

Will a guest who is not a Buddhist be expected to do anything other than sit?
Stand when others do so.

Are there any parts of the ceremony in which a guest who is not a Buddhist should *not* participate?
No.

If not disruptive to the ceremony, is it okay to:
◙ **Take pictures?** No.
◙ **Use a flash?** No.
◙ **Use a video camera?** No.
◙ **Use a tape recorder?** No.

Will contributions to the temple be collected at the ceremony?
No.

THE INTERMENT

Should guests attend the interment or cremation?
If so desired.

Whom should one ask for directions?
The funeral director or a monk or priest.

What happens at the graveside?
Prayers are recited and the body is committed to the ground.

Do guests who are not Buddhists participate at the graveside ceremony?
No.

COMFORTING THE BEREAVED

Is it appropriate to visit the home of the bereaved after the funeral?
Yes.

Will there be a religious service at the home of the bereaved?
In Cambodian, Thai and Ceylonese traditions, monks lead a "merit trans-ference" ceremony seven days after the burial or cremation. The purpose is to generate good energy for the deceased in his or her new incarnation.

Will food be served?

Yes.

How soon after the funeral will a mourner usually return to a normal work schedule?

This totally depends on the individual mourner. There are no religious prescriptions regarding refraining from work.

How soon after the funeral will a mourner usually return to a normal social schedule?

Usually not until three months after the death.

Are there mourning customs to which a friend who is not a Buddhist should be sensitive?

No.

Are there rituals for observing the anniversary of the death?

Japanese, Cambodian, Thai and Ceylonese traditions have a memorial service 90 days after the death. A year after the death, all four traditions have "merit transference" ceremonies, whose purpose is to generate good energy for the deceased in his or her new incarnation. These may be held either at the home of the bereaved or at a temple. Food will be served, since sharing is an integral part of all Buddhist ceremonies.

6

Christian and Missionary Alliance

HISTORY AND BELIEFS

The Christian and Missionary Alliance is literally an *alliance* of evangelical believers, who have joined together, through their local churches and their own personal lives, to bring the gospel and the life of Jesus Christ to all peoples and all nations.

In the United States, the denomination has its roots in two groups—the Christian Alliance and the Evangelical Missionary Alliance—both of which were founded in 1887 by Dr. Albert B. Simpson, a Presbyterian minister motivated by the spiritual needs of urban residents in the United States, as well as by the unevangelized peoples in other lands. These two organizations' underlying thrust was Jesus' comment in Matthew (24:14): "The gospel of the kingdom will be preached in the whole world as a testimony to all nations, and then the end will come." In Canada, a movement that was begun in 1887 by Rev. John Salmon joined the Christian Alliance in 1889, becoming the Auxiliary of the Christian Alliance, Toronto.

The two groups that had been founded by Dr. Simpson were combined in 1897 to form the Christian and Missionary Alliance, which now has a worldwide membership of 2.4 million and ministries devoted to evangelism for Christ in 56 countries and territories. In 1981, the Canadian districts became autonomous and formed the Christian and Missionary Alliance in Canada. Its General Assembly is held every two years.

Presently, more than 1,169 missionaries are taking the Christian gospel to almost 150 "unsaved people groups" around the globe. The church defines a "people group" as "a distinct group of individuals having no community of Christians able to evangelize its people without outside help." For example, the Church has two missionaries evangelizing Moslems residing in Great Britain, six to Chinese living in Australia, four to Native Americans living in urban areas in the United States, and two to North American Jews.

The Church believes that Jesus Christ is the living Word of God, the supreme Revelation of divine love, the sacrificial Lamb of God who alone provides salvation for humanity and every need of body and soul, and is the only hope for a world of lost people. Baptism and the Lord's Supper are recognized as the two ordinances of the Church. These are not related to individual salvation, but are outward signs of an inward commitment to Christ. Baptism by immersion is taught and practiced. The Lord's Supper is administered regularly in church services.

Church policies, which are set by an annual General Council, are administered by a 28-member Board of Managers and are implemented by the staff of the national office and district offices. Each local church sends its pastor and lay delegates to General Council and district conferences so it can have a voice in shaping policy.

U.S. churches: 1,850
U.S. membership: 311,600
(*data from the* 1998 Yearbook of American and Canadian Churches)

Canadian churches: 376
Canadian membership: 87,197
(*data from the* 1998 Yearbook of American and Canadian Churches)

FUNERALS AND MOURNING

The Christian and Missionary Alliance believes that in its spiritual aspects, death is a separation from God; in its physical aspects, it shows that man is mortal. Therefore, death is seen as the most fearsome of enemies since all humans must die.

Jesus came to give life both immediately and in the future. Christians are still mortal since they die physically, but they die "in Christ." By His death and His resurrection, Jesus conquered death and His victory becomes the believer's victory. As I Corinthians (15:57) states, "But thanks be to God! He gives us the victory through our Lord Jesus Christ!"

The ceremony may last 45 to 60 minutes.

BEFORE THE CEREMONY

How soon after the death does the funeral usually take place?

Within two to three days.

What should someone who is not a member of the Christian and Missionary Alliance do upon hearing of the death of a member of that faith?

Telephone or visit the bereaved. Let them know of your concern for them and offer any help you can give them.

APPROPRIATE ATTIRE

Men: A jacket and tie. No head covering is required.

Women: A dress. Hems need not reach below the knees nor must clothing cover the arms. Open-toed shoes and modest jewelry are permissible. No head covering is required.

Dark, somber colors are advised, but not required.

GIFTS

Is it appropriate to send flowers or make a contribution?

Yes. Flowers may be sent to the home of the bereaved upon hearing of the death, to the funeral itself, or to the home of the bereaved after the funeral.

The family may designate certain charities to which contributions may be donated.

Is it appropriate to send food?

Yes. Food may be sent to the home of the bereaved upon hearing of the death or after the funeral.

THE CEREMONY

Where will the ceremony take place?

Usually in a church.

When should guests arrive and where should they sit?

Arrive early. Usually ushers will advise you where to sit.

If arriving late, are there times when a guest should *not* enter the ceremony?

Do not enter while prayers are being recited.

Are there times when a guest should *not* leave the ceremony?

No.

Will the bereaved family be present at the church before the ceremony?

Possibly. If so, let them know of your concern for them and offer any help you can give.

Is there a traditional greeting for the family?

Offer your condolences.

Will there be an open casket?

Usually.

Is a guest expected to view the body?

This is optional.

What is appropriate behavior upon viewing the body?

Spend a few moments in silence as you stand in front of the casket.

Who are the major officiants at the ceremony and what do they do?

- *The pastor,* who will officiate.
- *The musicians,* who will provide music.

What books are used?

A hymnal and Bible. The autonomy of individual churches precludes having standard hymnals and Bibles throughout the Church.

To indicate the order of the ceremony:

A program will be provided.

Will a guest who is not a member of the Christian and Missionary Alliance be expected to do anything other than sit?

No.

Are there any parts of the ceremony in which a guest who is not a member of the Christian and Missionary Alliance should *not* participate?

No.

If not disruptive to the ceremony, is it okay to:

- **Take pictures?** No.
- **Use a flash?** No.
- **Use a video camera?** No.
- **Use a tape recorder?** Yes.

Will contributions to the church be collected at the ceremony?

No.

THE INTERMENT

Should guests attend the interment?

Yes.

Whom should one ask for directions?

Ask the ushers.

What happens at the graveside?

Prayers are recited, Scripture is read and a short service is held.

Do guests who are not members of the Christian and Missionary Alliance participate at the graveside ceremony?

They may participate if requested to do so by the family.

COMFORTING THE BEREAVED

Is it appropriate to visit the home of the bereaved after the funeral?

Yes, but limit your visit to 30 minutes or less.

Will there be a religious service at the home of the bereaved?

Very rarely is a service held at home.

Will food be served?

Yes, but no alcoholic beverages.

How soon after the funeral will a mourner usually return to a normal work schedule?

This is entirely at the discretion of the bereaved.

How soon after the funeral will a mourner usually return to a normal social schedule?

This is entirely at the discretion of the bereaved.

Are there mourning customs to which a friend who is not a member of the Christian and Missionary Alliance should be sensitive?

No.

Are there rituals for observing the anniversary of the death?

No.

7

Christian Church (Disciples of Christ)

HISTORY AND BELIEFS

Reacting against the sectarianism common among religions on the American frontier of the early 1800s, the founders of the Christian Church urged a union of all Christians. Two independently developing groups, the "Disciples" and the "Christians," formally united in 1832.

They advocated adult baptism by immersion, weekly observance of the Lord's Supper (more commonly known as communion) and autonomy of local congregations.

The Canadian church traces its heritage to this new American group and to a similar movement within the Scotch Baptist movement in Britain.

One joins the Church after simply declaring his or her faith in Jesus and being baptized by immersion. The highly ecumenical Church was among the founders of the National and the World Councils of Churches. Its secular-oriented programs focus on such issues as helping the mentally retarded, aiding war victims, bolstering farms and improving cities and education.

The Church is highly democratic. Local congregations own their own property and control their budgets and programs. Each congregation votes in the General Assembly that meets every two years.

U.S. churches: 3,840
U.S. membership: 910,000
(data from the 1998 Yearbook of American and Canadian Churches*)*

Canadian churches: 34
Canadian membership: 3,286
(data from the 1998 Yearbook of American and Canadian Churches*)*

FUNERALS AND MOURNING

For Disciples of Christ, death is not the end of life, but the beginning of new life. While Disciples will grieve, they do not mourn as do those who have no hope of ever seeing the deceased again or who are without the sure hope that those who die in faith in Jesus Christ are assured eternal life with God.

The funeral is a service in itself. A pastor presides. Pall bearers carry or push the casket on rollers into the funeral home or church sanctuary.

The service will last between 15 and 30 minutes. All attending are expected to remain to the end.

BEFORE THE CEREMONY

How soon after the death does the funeral usually take place?
Within one week.

What should someone who is not a Disciple of Christ do upon hearing of the death of a member of that faith?
Call the bereaved or visit or send a note to express your sympathy at their loss. Express your concern for them

APPROPRIATE ATTIRE

Men: Jacket and tie. No head covering is required.

Women: A dress or skirt and blouse are acceptable. Open-toed shoes and modest jewelry are fine. No head covering is required.

Dark, somber colors are recommended.

GIFTS

Is it appropriate to send flowers or make a contribution?
It is appropriate to send flowers unless the family expresses otherwise. Send them to the deceased's home or to the funeral home where the funeral will be held.

It is also appropriate to make a donation in memory of the deceased. The family will often announce, either through the funeral home or a classified ad in a local newspaper, the preferred cause or charity for memorial contributions.

There is no standard amount to be donated.

Is it appropriate to send food?
You may want to send food to the home of the bereaved for the family and their guests.

THE CEREMONY

Where will the ceremony take place?
Either in the church of the deceased or a funeral home.

When should guests arrive and where should they sit?
It is customary to arrive early enough to be seated when the service begins. Someone will tell you where and when to sit.

If arriving late, are there times when a guest should *not* enter the ceremony?
Do not enter during the procession or during prayer.

Will the bereaved family be present at the church or funeral home before the ceremony?
There is often a visitation at the funeral home the night before the service.

Is there a traditional greeting for the family?
Express your sorrow and regrets.

Will there be an open casket?
Usually.

Is a guest expected to view the body?
This is entirely optional.

What is appropriate behavior upon viewing the body?
Stand quietly near the casket, view the body and extend your condolences to the family.

Who are the major officiants at the ceremony and what do they do?
▪ *The pastor*, who presides.

What books are used?
The New Standard Revised Version of the Bible (New York: National Council of Churches' Division of Christian Education, 1989).

To indicate the order of the ceremony:
A program will be distributed.

Will a guest who is not a Disciple of Christ be expected to do anything other than sit?
The level of participation depends on whether or not the guest is Christian. Christians will generally be expected to stand and sing with congregants and read prayers aloud. Non-Christians are expected to stand with congregants and are invited to sing and pray with them.

Are there are any parts of the service in which a guest who is not a Disciple of Christ should *not* participate?
No, unless these parts violate or compromise their own religious beliefs.

If not disruptive to the ceremony, it is okay to:
- **Take pictures?** No.
- **Use a flash?** No.
- **Use a video camera?** No.
- **Use a tape recorder?** No.

Will contributions to the church be collected at the ceremony?
No.

THE INTERMENT

Should guests attend the interment?
This is optional. If one decides to do so, join the funeral procession.

Whom should one ask for directions?
The funeral director.

What happens at the graveside?
The casket is carried to the grave. Prayers and readings are offered. The pastor blesses the earth placed on the casket.

Do guests who are not Disciples of Christ participate at the graveside service?
No, they are simply present.

COMFORTING THE BEREAVED

Is it appropriate to visit the home of the bereaved after the funeral?
Yes. More than once is appropriate. The length of the visit depends on one's judgment and sensitivities.

Will there be a religious service at the home of the bereaved?
No.

Will food be served?
Yes. Wait for grace to be said before eating. It would not be considered impolite not to eat.

How soon after the funeral will a mourner usually return to a normal work schedule?
Within three days to a week.

How soon after the funeral will a mourner usually return to a normal social schedule?
Within three days to a week.

Are there mourning customs to which a friend who is not a Disciple of Christ should be sensitive?
No.

Are there rituals for observing the anniversary of the death?
No.

8

Christian Congregation

(Also known as The Christian Church.
Since local churches are semi-autonomous, they are sometimes known as
Independents or Universalists. This latter term should not
be confused with Unitarian Universalism.)

HISTORY AND BELIEFS

The Christian Congregation originated in the late 18th century along the frontier near the Ohio River. It was incorporated in 1887 when several ministers formally constituted the Church because they sought greater cooperation with each other.

The Church considers itself to be a progressive organization that places greater emphasis on ethical behavior than on strict adherence to doctrine. Its guiding principle is John 13:34-35: "A new commandment I give to you, that you love one another, even as I have loved you, that you also love one another. By this, all men will know that you are My disciples, if you have love for one another." Essential to Church belief is the conviction that all wars are unjust, and that war itself is an obsolete means to resolve disputes. Its doctrinal positions are intended to transcend racial distinctions and national identities and to foster a creative activism.

The Christian Congregation is an evangelistic association whose local churches are semi-autonomous.

Number of U.S. churches: 1,437
Number of U.S. members: 114,700
(data from the 1998 Yearbook of American and Canadian Churches)

FUNERALS AND MOURNING

The Christian Congregation affirms that, in faith, one can look forward to life with God after death. The Church does not believe that one necessarily has an immortal soul, but that one can become immortal by living an ethical life. If one does not achieve immortality, then he or she does not endure everlasting punishment in the equivalent of hell, but is eventually extinguished and ceases to exist in any form.

The funeral is a ceremony in itself and usually lasts about 15 to 30 minutes.

BEFORE THE CEREMONY

How soon after the death does the funeral usually take place?

Usually within two to three days.

What should someone who is not a member of The Christian Congregation do upon hearing of the death of a member of that faith?

Telephone or visit the bereaved. Express your condolences, and mostly listen to the mourner if that person wants to talk.

APPROPRIATE ATTIRE

Men: A jacket and tie. No head covering is required.

Women: A dress or a skirt and blouse. Arms do not have to be covered nor do hems have to be below the knees. Open-toed shoes and modest jewelry are permissible. No head covering is required.

There are no rules regarding colors of clothing, but somber, dark colors are recommended for men and women.

GIFTS

Is it appropriate to send flowers or make a contribution?

Flowers may be sent to the home of the bereaved. Contributions are optional, but are not ordinarily encouraged.

Is it appropriate to send food?

Yes. This may be sent to the home of the bereaved upon hearing of the news of the death or after the funeral.

THE CEREMONY

Where will the ceremony take place?

At a church or funeral home. Sometimes the funeral will be at the home of the bereaved.

When should guests arrive and where should they sit?

Arrive early. Ushers will advise guests where to sit.

If arriving late, are there times when a guest should *not* enter the ceremony?

Do not enter during prayer.

Will the bereaved family be present at the church or funeral home before the ceremony?

Possibly. If so, briefly express your condolences.

Will there be an open casket?

Usually.

Is a guest expected to view the body?

This is entirely optional.

What is appropriate behavior upon viewing the body?

Stand silently near the casket and view the body. You are seeing a friend for the last time in this earthly sphere.

Who are the major officiants at the ceremony and what do they do?

- *The minister,* who officiates.
- *Musicians or singers,* who provide music.

What books are used?

A hymnal and a Bible. (The Christian Congregation has no official Bible translation. Each church chooses the hymnal and the translation of the Bible it will use.)

To indicate the order of the ceremony:

A program will be provided or the officiating minister may make announcements.

Will a guest who is not a member of The Christian Congregation be expected to do anything other than sit?

No.

Are there any parts of the ceremony in which a guest who is not a member of The Christian Congregation should *not* participate?

No.

If not disruptive to the ceremony, is it okay to:

▪ **Take pictures?** Yes.
▪ **Use a flash camera?** No.
▪ **Use a video camera?** Yes.
▪ **Use a tape recorder?** Yes.

Will contributions to the church be collected at the ceremony?

No.

THE INTERMENT

Should guests attend the interment?

This is optional.

Whom should one ask for directions?

The funeral director.

What happens at the graveside?

Scriptures and prayers are recited by the minister and the body is committed to the ground.

Do guests who are not members of The Christian Congregation participate at the graveside ceremony?

No. They are simply present.

COMFORTING THE BEREAVED

Is it appropriate to visit the home of the bereaved after the funeral?

Yes, at any mutually convenient time. It is best to visit two or three days after the funeral. The length of the visit depends on your closeness to the bereaved. Typically, one stays about 20 to 30 minutes.

Will there be a religious service at the home of the bereaved?

No.

Will food be served?

This is unlikely. What is certain is that no alcoholic beverages will be served.

How soon after the funeral will a mourner usually return to a normal work schedule?

Usually within three days after the funeral.

How soon after the funeral will a mourner usually return to a normal social schedule?

Usually within a week after the funeral.

Are there mourning customs to which a friend who is not a member of The Christian Congregation should be sensitive?

No.

Are there rituals for observing the anniversary of the death?

No.

9

Christian Science
(Church of Christ, Scientist)

HISTORY AND BELIEFS

Christian Science was founded in 1879 by Mary Baker Eddy, who was healed of a serious injury in 1866 while reading an account in the New Testament of Jesus' healings. Thirteen years later, she established the Church of Christ, Scientist, in Boston. Mrs. Eddy died in 1910.

The church consists of the Mother Church—the First Church of Christ, Scientist—in Boston and approximately 2,400 branch churches in about 63 countries around the world.

Christian Science theology holds that God created man in His image and likeness. Christian Scientists also believe that God is good and that His creation is all that is real and eternal. This belief is based on the first chapter of Genesis, which states: "So God created man in His own image, in the image of God created He him; male and female created He them.... And God saw everything that He had made, and, behold, it was good."

Therefore, Christian Scientists believe that sin, disease and death do not originate in God. Rather, they are considered to be distortions of the human mind.

The church is grounded in the teachings of the King James Bible and relies on spiritual means for healing. According to the church, its spiritual healing "is not popular faith healing or human mind cure. It is not self-hypnosis, mere positive thinking, autosuggestion, or spontaneous remission. Nor is it to be confused with Scientology or New Age thinking...."

"Christian Scientists find the Christian healing they experience is the reinstatement of the healing method practiced by Jesus 2,000 years ago. It is based on understanding the laws of God revealed in the Bible, and conforming to them. These laws are available for all mankind to practice and, thereby, obtain full salvation from sickness as well as sin.

"Christian Science healing involves more than healing sick bodies. It heals broken hearts and minds as well as broken homes, and is directly applicable to all of society's ills."

U.S. churches: 2,400
U.S. membership: Not available
(data from the 1998 Yearbook of American and Canadian Churches*)*

Canadian churches: 94
Canadian membership: Not available

FUNERALS AND MOURNING

According to Christian Science teaching, the church does not designate special arrangements or rituals for funerals or mourning. A funeral service is optional.

BEFORE THE CEREMONY

How soon after the death does the funeral usually take place?
Usually about two to four days.

What should someone who is not a Christian Scientist do upon hearing of the death of a member of that faith?
Telephone or visit the bereaved or send a condolence card or personal letter.

APPROPRIATE ATTIRE

Men: A jacket and tie. No head covering is required.

Women: A dress, a skirt and blouse or a pants suit. Arms do not have to be covered by clothing nor do hems need to reach below the knees. Modest jewelry and open-toed shoes are permissible. No head covering is required.

There are no rules regarding colors of clothing, but slightly subdued colors are preferable.

GIFTS

Is it appropriate to send flowers or make a contribution?
Both flowers to the bereaved family and contributions in the name of the deceased are appropriate. Flowers may be sent to the homes of the bereaved. Contributions are often made to the church of the deceased.

Is it appropriate to send food?
Yes, any kind.

THE CEREMONY

Where does the ceremony take place?
Christian Science churches are used only for public worship services. Private funeral or memorial services are arranged by the families concerned and are usually held in their own homes or in funeral homes.

When should guests arrive and where should they sit?
Arrive early. Sit wherever you wish.

If arriving late, are there times when a guest should *not* enter the ceremony?
No.

Are there times when a guest should *not* leave the ceremony?
No.

Will the bereaved family be present at the church or funeral home before the ceremony?
This depends on the family's wishes.

Is there a traditional greeting for the family?
No.

Will there be an open casket?
Rarely. While most Christian Scientists do not have open viewing at the memorial service, this is done at the discretion of the individual.

Who are the major officiants at the ceremony and what do they do?
Since the Christian Science church has no clergy, the service is conducted by a Christian Scientist who might be a Reader or a Christian Science practitioner or teacher, or a friend of the deceased.

(A "practitioner" is an experienced Christian Scientist who, on a professional basis, devotes full time to the healing ministry. Individuals enter the public practice of Christian Science as a life work only after demonstrating a consistent ability to heal others through Christian Scientific prayer.)

What books are used?

The format and content of a Christian Science funeral service are determined by the family or whoever conducts the service. However, the service typically consists of readings from the King James Bible and from *Science and Health with Key to the Scriptures* or some other writing by Mrs. Eddy. Silent prayer, followed by those attending repeating the Lord's Prayer, may also be included. If music is desired, the Christian Science Hymnal contains hymns suitable for funerals.

The service usually includes no personal remarks or eulogy, but the family's wishes are taken into account. If they request, a poem or hymn that is not in the Christian Science Hymnal may be read or sung.

Will a guest who is not a Christian Scientist be expected to do anything other than sit?

No.

Are there any parts of the ceremony in which a guest who is not a Christian Scientist should *not* participate?

No.

If not disruptive to the ceremony, is it okay to:

- Take pictures? No.
- Use a flash camera? No.
- Use a video camera? No.
- Use a tape recorder? No.

Will contributions to the church be collected at the ceremony?

No.

THE INTERMENT

Cremation or burial is solely the bereaved family's decision.

COMFORTING THE BEREAVED

Is it appropriate to visit the home of the bereaved after the funeral?

Yes.

Will there be a religious service at the home of the bereaved?

No.

Will food be served?

Sometimes, but not alcoholic beverages.

How soon after the funeral will a mourner usually return to a normal work schedule?

This is solely an individual decision. Christian Scientists do not have a prescribed period of mourning or specific customs of mourning.

How soon after the funeral will a mourner usually return to a normal social schedule?

This is solely an individual decision. Christian Scientists do not have a prescribed period of mourning or specific customs of mourning.

Are there rituals for observing the anniversary of the death?

No.

10

Church of the Brethren

HISTORY AND BELIEFS

The Church of the Brethren began in 1708 in an obscure German princi pality, Sayn-Wittgenstein-Hohenstein, when five men and three women pledged to base their lives on biblical lessons and truths and "to take up all the commandments of Jesus Christ as an easy yoke." They criticized the Church as inattentive to the Bible and too concerned with maintaining itself as an institution. They also believed that baptism was not for infants, but for believers who had reached a mature age of accountability and could decide for themselves to embrace Christian precepts.

By denying the validity of the baptism each member of this small group had received as infants, they implicitly challenged the authority of the existing Church. Since churches in Germany were closely identified with the state, adult baptism was considered to be not only religious heresy, but also treason. Soon, members of this expanding group were persecuted by the state, not only for their stance on baptism, but also because they refused to take oaths or serve in the military.

In 1719, some Brethren fled Europe for Pennsylvania. Four years later, the entire male membership in the Germantown, Pennsylvania, congregation began an evangelistic mission to preach, baptize and form new congregations throughout the colonies. By the middle of the next century, there were new churches as far as California.

The original members of the Church in Germany had simply called themselves "brethren," which meant brothers and sisters. But in 1836, legal papers in the United States listed the group as the Fraternity of German Baptists. This became the German Baptist Brethren in 1871, although they were also nicknamed "Dunkers" because of adult baptism by immersion.

In 1908, the German identification disappeared and the name was changed to the Church of the Brethren. There have been recent murmurings about again changing the Church's name since "brethren" generally refers only to males in today's usage. For now, "brethren" is being retained to remind members of the deep connections they have—as sisters and brothers—in their faith.

Church members affirm their belief in Jesus Christ as the Lord and Savior and promise to turn from sin and live in faithfulness to God and to the Church, taking Jesus as their model. The Church insists that members not thoughtlessly adopt the habits and ways of others, and encourages members to think carefully about how to live comfortably, but not ostentatiously, in an affluent society; to be aware of the environment and limited resources in a global community; and to engage in creative efforts to achieve peace and reconciliation. The Church condemns gambling and urges members to refrain from alcohol, drug and tobacco use. Brethren are encouraged to practice nonresistance in the face of violence, and discouraged from engaging in military service since the Church has declared all war to be sin.

Oath-taking is discouraged because the Church of the Brethren believes that Jesus advocated completely abolishing such practices (James 5:12) since persons should always be truthful, not just at particular moments. Taking an oath implies an erratic attitude toward truthfulness since it suggests that, this time, one is being truthful, yet is not truthful at other times. Jesus, according to the Church, taught that a true Christian knows the will of God and is true to it at all times. Indecisiveness, which is fostered by the devil, erodes one's credibility.

The Church also discourages members from resorting to civil court when injured by another because, as Peter Nead, the leading Brethren theologian of the 19th century, wrote, the doctrine taught by Jesus does not allow Christians "to retaliate or seek redress for their grievances. Under the law, retaliation was allowable, but not so under the Gospel of Jesus Christ." Instead, wrote Nead, when a Christian is injured by another, his only recourse is to suffer since that is what Jesus did and that is what anyone wishing to be a child of God must do.

But in a statement written in 1920, the Church slightly relaxed its proscription against members participating in proceedings in a civil court. The statement cited Matthew 5:40-41 and Luke 6:30 to show that Jesus taught that if the legal process cannot be avoided, then the Christian should do more than is required by secular law. The statement gave permission to

Brethren to comply with civil law if three preconditions were met: Such action did not violate such Christian principles as nonresistance; one Brethren had not resorted to civil law without the permission of another Brethren whom he was contesting in a court action; and the church's counsel is sought before resorting to civil law.

At least once a year, each church celebrates a "love feast," which may also be called an "agape (pronounced 'ah-GAH-pay') meal." The ceremony includes a mutual footwashing between two congregants of the same gender, who then embrace and give each other a "holy kiss." This is followed by communion and a simple meal. The ritual echoes Jesus' washing of the feet of His disciples at the Last Supper, where He sought to draw them closer into the fold of His love.

Individual Brethren congregations have considerable autonomy. Each sets its own budget and chooses its own pastor, a moderator who conducts the gatherings when Brethren meet to do church business, and a board of administration. Each also belongs to one of the 23 districts that comprise the Annual Conference, which meets each year to make decisions about the future of the Church. Each church can send at least one delegate to the conference.

U.S. churches: 1,106
U.S. membership: 141,800
(data from the 1998 *Yearbook of American and Canadian Churches)*

FUNERALS AND MOURNING

The Brethren funeral service or memorial service celebrates the resurrection promised by Jesus Christ: "I am the resurrection and the life. Those who believe in Me, even though they die, will live, and everyone who lives and believes in Me will never die."

The service also celebrates the individual who has died, and is an opportunity to reflect upon the meaning of his or her life.

The funeral ceremony is a ceremony in itself and may last about 30 to 60 minutes.

BEFORE THE CEREMONY

How soon after the death does the funeral or memorial service usually take place?

Two to three days. If a memorial service is held instead of a funeral, it may be held from one to three weeks after the death itself.

What should someone who is not a member of the Church of the Brethren do upon hearing of the death of a member of that faith?

If the deceased was a close friend or a relative, telephone or visit the bereaved to express your condolences. If a "visitation" or a "wake" is scheduled, visit then if you can.

APPROPRIATE ATTIRE

Men: A jacket and tie or more casual attire, depending on local custom. No head covering is required.

Women: A dress or a skirt and blouse or a pants suit. Hems need not reach below the knees nor must clothing cover the arms. Open-toed shoes and modest jewelry are permissible. No head covering is required.

There are no rules regarding colors of clothing.

GIFTS

Is it appropriate to send flowers or make a contribution?

Flowers may be sent to the funeral service or to the home of the bereaved upon hearing of the death of the deceased or before or after the funeral. In lieu of flowers, contributions may be made to a fund or charity designated by the family of the deceased.

Is it appropriate to send food?

Yes. This may be sent to the home of the bereaved upon hearing of the death or after the funeral.

THE CEREMONY

Where will the ceremony take place?

In a church or a funeral home.

When should guests arrive and where should they sit?

Arrive at the time for which the ceremony has been called. Ushers may advise guests where to sit. If there are no ushers, sit wherever you wish.

If arriving late, are there times when a guest should *not* enter the ceremony?

Ushers will advise you when to enter.

Will the bereaved family be present at the church before the ceremony?

Possibly.

Is there a traditional greeting for the family?

Just express your sympathy for the bereaved.

Will there be an open casket?

Possibly.

Is a guest expected to view the body?

This is entirely optional.

What is appropriate behavior upon viewing the body?

Be quiet and respectful. Gaze silently at the deceased for a brief moment.

Who are the major officiants at the ceremony and what do they do?

- *The pastor,* who officiates.
- *The eulogist(s),* who delivers a eulogy about the deceased.
- *A choir, a vocal ensemble, or a soloist,* who may be present to sing.
- *An organist or a pianist,* who provides music.

What books are used?

Since each congregation chooses the translation of the Bible it will use, different translations are used throughout the Church. Among the more common translations used is the New Revised Standard Version. Also used will be *Hymnal: A Worship Book* (Elgin, Ill.: Brethren Press, 1992).

To indicate the order of the ceremony:

A program may be provided.

Will a guest who is not a member of the Church of the Brethren be expected to do anything other than sit?

No. It is entirely optional for guests to stand, kneel, read prayers aloud and sing with members of the congregation.

Are there any parts of the ceremony in which a guest who is not a member of the Church of the Brethren should *not* participate?

No.

If not disruptive to the ceremony, is it okay to:

- **Take pictures?** No.
- **Use a flash?** No.

▪ **Use a video camera?** No.

▪ **Use a tape recorder?** Only with prior approval of the bereaved.

Will contributions to the church be collected at the ceremony?

No.

THE INTERMENT

Should guests attend the interment?

This is entirely optional.

Whom should one ask for directions?

The funeral director or a member of the family of the deceased.

What happens at the graveside?

Scripture is read, usually Isaiah 40:6b, 8 or 66:13; or Psalm 46:1–2a, 103:13–14, or 121:1–2, 7b–8. Prayers are then invoked and the body is committed to the ground.

Do guests who are not members of the Church of the Brethren participate at the graveside ceremony?

No. They are simply present.

COMFORTING THE BEREAVED

Is it appropriate to visit the home of the bereaved after the funeral?

Yes. It is recommended that the visit be brief. When visiting, express your sympathy to the bereaved and offer specific help to them.

Will there be a religious service at the home of the bereaved?

This is rare.

Will food be served?

In many congregations, a fellowship meal is served in the church to guests, family, and friends after the funeral or memorial service.

How soon after the funeral will a mourner usually return to a normal work schedule?

This varies according to one's personal needs. There is no doctrine on mourning.

How soon after the funeral will a mourner usually return to a normal social schedule?

This varies according to one's personal needs. There is no doctrine on mourning.

Are there mourning customs to which a friend who is not a member of the Church of the Brethren should be sensitive?

No, but the thoughtful and compassionate reflections of friends are encouraged.

Are there rituals for observing the anniversary of the death?

No.

11

Church of the Nazarene

HISTORY AND BELIEFS

The distant roots of Church of the Nazarene are in Methodism; its more recent roots are in the teachings of John Wesley, who led a revival centered around the doctrines of holiness and sanctification in 18th-century England; and its most recent roots are in three churches that merged in 1907 and 1908: The Association of Pentecostal Churches, which was based in New York and New England; the Holiness Church of Christ, which was based in the South; and the Church of the Nazarene, based in California.

The church's doctrine centers around "sanctification," which is a feeling of grace stemming from "regeneration." This latter term refers to the sense of being made anew through faith in Jesus Christ. All pastors (who may also be called "ministers") and local church officials must profess this experience. Other prime doctrines are that the Scriptures contain all truths necessary to Christian faith and living; that through His death, Christ atoned for the sins of humanity; and that upon Christ's return, the dead will be resurrected.

Tobacco and alcohol use are prohibited. Church members believe in divine healing, but not to the exclusion of medical aid.

Each of the Church's 85 districts in the United States and Canada is supervised by a district superintendent, who is elected for a four-year term by members of the district assembly. Internationally, the Church is administered by a general board, which consists of an equal number of lay members and ministers.

The Church emphasizes evangelism, and more than 650 missionaries conduct missionary work around the globe.

Worldwide, there are almost 850,000 Nazarenes (as members of the Church of the Nazarene are called) in more than 8,600 churches.

U.S. churches: 5,135
U.S. membership: 608,000
(data from the 1998 Yearbook of American and Canadian Churches*)*

Canadian churches: 182
Canadian membership: 11,931
(data from the 1998 Yearbook of American and Canadian Churches*)*

FUNERALS AND MOURNING

The Church of the Nazarene affirms that life is eternal and that, through faith in Christ, one can look forward to life with God after death. Death may be a time of separation from the body, but the soul and new body will be reunited upon the coming of Christ and the final judgment. Funerals have as their purposes: 1) expressing grief and comforting one another in our bereavement; 2) celebrating the life of the deceased; and 3) affirming faith in life with God after death. Which of these is most emphasized at the funeral depends on the circumstances of the death and the extent of the faith of the deceased.

The funeral lasts about 30 to 60 minutes.

BEFORE THE CEREMONY

How soon after the death does the funeral usually take place?

Within three to six days.

What should a non-Nazarene do upon hearing of the death of a member of that faith?

Express your condolences to the bereaved family through a telephone call or a card or letter.

APPROPRIATE ATTIRE

Men: A suit and tie or a sport jacket, slacks and a tie. No head covering is required.

Women: A dress or a business suit. Arms do not have to be covered nor do hems need to reach below the knees. Open-toed shoes and modest jewelry are permissible. No head covering is required.

Dark, somber colors are recommended.

GIFTS

Is it appropriate to send flowers or make a contribution?

Yes. Often family members request that such contributions be made to the deceased's favorite charity in memory of the deceased.

Is it appropriate to send food?

Those who are especially close to the bereaved family often do so.

THE CEREMONY

Where will the ceremony take place?

In the church sanctuary or a funeral home.

When should guests arrive and where should they sit?

Arrive a few minutes before the time for which the service has been called. An usher will suggest where to sit.

If arriving late, are there times when a guest should *not* enter the ceremony?

Ushers will advise you when to enter.

Will the bereaved family be present at the church or funeral home before the ceremony?

Members of the bereaved family will arrive shortly before the funeral begins.

Is there a traditional greeting for the family?

Sincerely express your love and sympathy.

Will there be an open casket?

This is done entirely at the option of the family.

Is a guest expected to view the body?

No. One may exit the location of the funeral without passing by an open casket.

What is appropriate behavior upon viewing the body?

Pause briefly in front of the casket.

Who are the major officiants at the ceremony and what do they do?

- *The pastor(s),* who direct the service.
- *The musician(s),* who provide music.

What books are used?

For the funeral ceremony, only the pastor uses a book.

To indicate the order of the ceremony:

A program may be provided.

Will a guest who is not a Nazarene be expected to do anything other than sit?

No.

Are there any parts of the ceremony in which a guest who is not a Nazarene should *not* participate?

No.

If not disruptive to the ceremony, is it okay to:

◗ **Take pictures?** Only with prior permission of the pastor.
◗ **Use a flash?** Only with prior permission of the pastor.
◗ **Use a video camera?** Only with prior permission of the pastor.
◗ **Use a tape recorder?** Only with prior permission of the pastor.

Will contributions to the church be collected at the ceremony?

No.

THE INTERMENT

Should guests attend the interment?

Yes, unless it is announced that it will be a private interment.

Whom should one ask for directions?

The funeral director.

What happens at the graveside?

Prayers and words of committal are recited. Sometimes a song is sung.

Do guests who are not Nazarenes participate at the graveside ceremony?

No. The officiating pastor is the only participant.

COMFORTING THE BEREAVED

Is it appropriate to visit the home of the bereaved after the funeral?

Yes.

Will there be a religious service at the home of the bereaved?

No.

Will food be served?

No.

How soon after the funeral will a mourner usually return to a normal work schedule?

Absence from work is at the sole discretion of the mourner, but usually a few days, depending upon individual preference.

How soon after the funeral will a mourner usually return to a normal social schedule?

Absence from socializing is at the sole discretion of the mourner, but usually a few days, depending upon individual preference.

Are there mourning customs to which a friend who is not a Nazarene should be sensitive?

No.

Are there rituals for observing the anniversary of the death?

No.

12
Churches of Christ

HISTORY AND BELIEFS

Churches of Christ are autonomous congregations; there are no central governing offices or officers, and Church publications and institutions are either under local congregational control or independent of any one congregation. Members of the Churches of Christ appeal to the Bible alone to determine matters involving their faith and practice.

In the 19th century, Churches of Christ shared a common fellowship with the Christian Churches/Churches of Christ and with the Christian Church (Disciples of Christ). This relationship became strained after the Civil War because of emerging theories of interpreting the Bible and the centralizing of church-wide activities through a missionary society.

The Church teaches that Jesus Christ was divine, that the remission of sins can be achieved only by immersing oneself into Christ, and that the Scriptures were divinely inspired.

U.S. churches: 14,000
U. S. membership: 2.25 million
(data from the 1998 Yearbook of American and Canadian Churches*)*

Canadian churches: 145
Canadian membership: 6,950
(data from the 1998 Yearbook of American and Canadian Churches*)*

FUNERALS AND MOURNING

Members of the Churches of Christ believe that, upon death, the souls of those who are faithful Christians are taken to a place called Paradise to await the Final Judgment. The souls of those who are unfaithful or are not Christians are taken to a place called Tartarus to await judgment. On Judgment Day (which is the second coming of Jesus), the faithful will be taken to heaven and the unfaithful to hell.

The funeral service usually lasts about 30 minutes.

BEFORE THE CEREMONY

How soon after the death does the funeral usually take place?
Usually within two to three days. If family members cannot arrive for the funeral immediately, it may be delayed for four or five days. But this is rare.

What should someone who is not a member of the Churches of Christ do upon hearing of the death of a member of that faith?
Visit or telephone the bereaved before the funeral.

APPROPRIATE ATTIRE

Men: Jacket and tie. No head covering is required.

Women: A dress or a skirt and blouse. Hems slightly above the knees are fine. Open-toed shoes and modest jewelry are permissible. No head covering is required.

There are no rules regarding colors of clothing, but black or other somber colors or patterns are recommended.

GIFTS

Is it appropriate to send flowers or make a contribution?
Flowers, plants and cards are appropriate. They may be sent upon hearing the news of the death or shortly thereafter. They may be sent to the home of the deceased before or after the funeral, or to the funeral home before the funeral.

Contributions are not customary unless the family indicates they are appropriate.

Is it appropriate to send food?
Yes, to the home of the bereaved before or after the funeral.

THE CEREMONY

Where will the ceremony take place?
At a church or a funeral home.

When should guests arrive and where should they sit?

Arrive early. Register upon entry. No one will tell guests where to sit. Sit wherever there is an available seat.

If arriving late, are there times when a guest should *not* enter the ceremony?

Do not enter when the family is entering.

Will the bereaved family be present at the church or funeral home before the ceremony?

Yes, but there is no formal receiving line before the service.

Is there a traditional greeting for the family?

Express your condolences.

Will there be an open casket?

Usually.

Is a guest expected to view the body?

This is optional.

What is appropriate behavior upon viewing the body?

Most will pause briefly to look one last time at their friend or loved one. Occasionally, someone may pat the hand of the deceased or place a flower in the casket.

Who are the major officiants at the ceremony and what do they do?

- *One or more ministers* will deliver eulogies.
- *Singers* will lead songs.

What books are used?

A hymnal and a Bible (which includes the Old and New Testaments). The most commonly used hymnal is *Songs of the Church*. Others are *Majestic Hymnal* (Austin, Tex.: Firm Foundation Publishing, 1959) and *Songs of Faith and Praise* (West Monroe, La.: Alton Howard Publishers, 1993). The church does not endorse a particular version of the Bible.

Often, several different translations of the Bible are used by congregants at the same service. It is suggested that guests bring their own Bible.

To indicate the order of the ceremony:

The minister or funeral director will explain any involvement by those present and cue them should they be asked to do anything, such as view the body.

Will a guest who is not a member of the Churches of Christ be expected to do anything other than sit?
Guests may sing with the congregation, if the words are not contrary to their religious beliefs. Otherwise, nothing is expected of them.

Are there any parts of the ceremony in which a guest who is not a member of the Churches of Christ should *not* participate?
No.

If not disruptive to the ceremony, is it okay to:
◘ **Take pictures?** No.
◘ **Use a flash?** No.
◘ **Use a video camera?** No.
◘ **Use a tape recorder?** Yes.

Will contributions to the church be collected at the ceremony?
No.

THE INTERMENT

Should guests attend the interment?
Their attendance is optional.

Whom should one ask for directions?
The funeral director.

What happens at the graveside?
There is prayer, readings from the scriptures, and the minister gives comments about the deceased.

Do guests who are not members of the Churches of Christ participate at the graveside ceremony?
No. They are simply present.

COMFORTING THE BEREAVED

Is it appropriate to visit the home of the bereaved after the funeral?
Yes, either after the service at the cemetery or later.

Will there be a religious service at the home of the bereaved?
No.

Will food be served?
Possibly, but no alcoholic beverages.

How soon after the funeral will a mourner usually return to a normal work schedule?

Usually, the bereaved can be expected to return to work after one week of mourning.

How soon after the funeral will a mourner usually return to a normal social schedule?

Social occasions are usually avoided for about one month after the death, but this depends on the individual mourner.

Are there rituals for observing the anniversary of the death?

There is no formal ritual, although occasionally friends or relatives may call or visit each other on the anniversary of the death.

13

Episcopalian and Anglican

HISTORY AND BELIEFS

The Episcopal/Anglican Church is derived from the Church of England and shares with it traditions of faith as set forth in its *Book of Common Prayer*.

The English settlers who settled in Jamestown, Virginia, in 1607 brought the seeds of the Episcopal Church to America. After the American Revolution, the Church became independent from the Anglican Church and adopted the name of the Protestant Episcopal Church in the United States of America. This was shortened in 1967 when the Episcopal Church became the Church's official alternate name.

To many Americans after the Revolution, the Church was suspect because it had been closely linked with the British Crown and because many of its leaders and members had sided with England during the war. But extensive missionary efforts in the fledgling nation's new territories (as well as in Africa, Latin America and the Far East) and an eventual network of dioceses from the Atlantic to the Pacific helped it to finally establish its own identity.

In Canada, the first known service was performed by a chaplain in Sir Martin Frobisher's expedition in Frobisher Bay on September 2, 1578. In subsequent years, Anglicanism spread as a result of immigration from the British Isles and the coming of Loyalists, many of whom were Anglicans, after the American Revolution.

The Church is a fairly non-doctrinaire institution. It teaches that the Holy Scriptures were written by people, and inspired by the Holy Spirit (the empowering spirit of God), and that reason helps members penetrate to the full depths of God's truths. It does not control interpretation and practice, and urges members to make responsible moral decisions under the guidance of scripture, tradition and ordained ministry and in response to sincere prayer.

The Episcopal/Anglican Church is democratically structured. Each diocese, which consists of a group of parishes (or churches), is presided over by a bishop, who is democratically elected by a diocesan synod.

According to *The Book of Common Prayer*, "the duty of all Christians is to follow Christ, to come together week by week for corporate worship; and to work, pray and give for the spread of the Kingdom of God."

U.S. churches: 7,415
U.S. membership: 2.5 million
(data from the 1998 Yearbook of American and Canadian Churches*)*

Canadian churches: 2,390
Canadian membership: 740,262

FUNERALS AND MOURNING

In the Episcopal/Anglican Church, a funeral service can be either part of a larger service or a ceremony in itself. If it is part of a larger service, that service is called a "requiem," which includes a Holy Communion service.

Episcopalians/Anglicans believe that Christ will come and judge all, the living and dead. Some will be consigned to heaven, where they will spend eternal life in the enjoyment of God. Others will be consigned to hell, where they will spend eternal death in the rejection of God.

BEFORE THE CEREMONY

How soon after the death does the funeral usually take place?
Usually within two to three days.

What should a non-Episcopalian/Anglican do upon hearing of the death of a member of that faith?
Telephone or visit the bereaved. There is no specific "ritual" for calling or expressing sympathy to someone who is mourning.

APPROPRIATE ATTIRE

Men: Jacket and tie. No head covering is required.

Women: A dress. Clothing should be modest, with arms covered and hems below the knee. Open-toed shoes and modest jewelry are permissible. No head covering is required.

Somber colors are recommended for clothing.

GIFTS

Is it appropriate to send flowers or make a contribution?
Frequently, obituary notices will indicate if flowers are appropriate and may list specific charities for which contributions can be made in memory of the deceased.

Is it appropriate to send food?
Ask the bereaved.

THE CEREMONY

Where will the ceremony take place?
At a church or a funeral home.

When should guests arrive and where should they sit?
Arrive early. Sit wherever you choose.

If arriving late, are there times when a guest should *not* enter the ceremony?
No.

Will the bereaved family be present at the church or funeral home before the service?
Yes.

Is there a traditional greeting for the family?
No.

Will there be an open casket?
Rarely.

Is a guest expected to view the body?
This is entirely optional.

What is appropriate behavior upon viewing the body?
A moment of silent prayer.

Who are the major officiants at the ceremony and what do they do?
◘ *A priest*, who leads the service.

What books are used?

The Book of Common Prayer (New York: Church Hymnal Corp., 1986) and a hymnal. In Canada, *The Book of Alternative Services* (Toronto: The Anglican Book Center, 1985) may be used. Occasionally, the Bible lessons are included in the program.

To indicate the order of the ceremony:

A program will be provided.

Will a guest who is not Episcopalian/Anglican be expected to do anything other than sit?

They are expected to stand and kneel with the congregation, read prayers aloud and sing with congregants, if this does not compromise their personal beliefs. If one does not wish to kneel, sit when congregants do so.

Are there any parts of the ceremony in which a guest who is not Episcopalian/Anglican should *not* participate?

Do not receive communion or say any prayers contradictory to the beliefs of your own faith. Only baptized Christians may receive communion.

If not disruptive to the ceremony, is it okay to:

- **Take pictures?** No.
- **Use a flash?** No.
- **Use a video camera?** No.
- **Use a tape recorder?** No.

Will contributions to the church be collected at the ceremony?

No.

THE INTERMENT

Should guests attend the interment?

Yes, especially if the deceased was a close friend.

Whom should one ask for directions?

The funeral director or another guest.

What happens at the graveside?

The body is committed to the ground. If there has been a cremation, the ashes are either buried or put in a vault.

Do guests who are not Episcopalian/Anglicans participate at the graveside ceremony?

No. They are simply present.

COMFORTING THE BEREAVED

Is it appropriate to visit the home of the bereaved after the funeral?

Yes, although there is no specific "ritual" for calling or expressing sympathy to someone who is mourning. Nor is there a "ritual" that guides the behavior of the mourners.

Will there be a religious service at the home of the bereaved?

No.

Will food be served?

This is at the discretion of the bereaved.

How soon after the funeral will a mourner usually return to a normal work schedule?

One week.

How soon after the funeral will a mourner usually return to a normal social schedule?

This is entirely at the discretion of the bereaved.

14

Evangelical Free Church

HISTORY AND BELIEFS

The Evangelical Free Church is an association of autonomous churches that are united by a commitment to serve Jesus Christ. "Evangelical" refers to Church members' commitment to the proclamation of the Gospel and the authority of the Scriptures as the only sufficient guide to faith and practice. "Free" refers to the church government that assures local churches are independent of a central controlling body. Evangelical Free Churches depend upon the active participation of pastors and laity to make decisions that direct their local church.

The Evangelical Free Church of America was formed in 1950 by the merger of the Swedish Evangelical Free Church and the Norwegian-Danish Evangelical Free Church Association. The two denominations had a total of 275 local churches, and both had originated in the revival movements of the late nineteenth century.

A partner Church, The Evangelical Free Church of Canada, also of Scandinavian heritage, was incorporated under federal charter in 1967, although it traces its history to Enchant, Alberta, where the first formally organized congregation opened its doors in 1917.

From its inception, the Evangelical Free Church has been committed to being actively involved in the mission of Jesus Christ. Internationally, this dates from one of its two original Churches—the Swedish Evangelical Free Church—sending their first missionaries to China in 1887.

The Evangelical Free Church has national church bodies in 16 nations and plans to expand to another 15 countries. Domestically, the Church is committed to "planting" 1,000 new local churches by the year 2001.

U.S. churches: 1,224
U.S. membership: 242,619
(*data from the* 1998 Yearbook of American and Canadian Churches)

Canadian churches: 135
Canadian membership: 7,315
(*data from the* Evangelical Free Church of Canada 1998–1999 Directory)

FUNERALS AND MOURNING

Members of the Evangelical Free Church believe that upon the coming of Jesus Christ, the dead will be resurrected, and believers will receive everlasting blessedness and unbelievers will receive everlasting conscious punishment.

A ceremony in itself, the funeral service lasts about 30 and 60 minutes.

BEFORE THE CEREMONY

How soon after the death does the funeral usually take place?

Usually within two to three days, but sometimes as long as one week.

What should one who is not a member of the Evangelical Free Church do upon hearing of the death of a member of that faith?

Telephone or visit the bereaved and express one's condolences and concern.

APPROPRIATE ATTIRE

Men: A jacket and tie. No head covering is required.

Women: A dress or a skirt and blouse. Open-toed shoes and modest jewelry are permissible. Clothing need not cover the arms nor hems reach below the knees. No head covering is required.

There are no rules regarding colors of clothing, but dark, somber colors are recommended.

GIFTS

Is it appropriate to send flowers or make a contribution?

Yes. Flowers may be sent to the home of the bereaved upon hearing of the death, or they may be sent to the funeral home or the church where the funeral will be held. Contributions may be made to a memorial fund designated by family members.

Is it appropriate to send food?

Yes. This may be sent to the home of the bereaved.

THE CEREMONY

Where will the ceremony take place?

Either in a church or a funeral home.

When should guests arrive and where should they sit?

Arrive early. Ushers usually advise guests where to sit.

If arriving late, are there times when a guest should *not* enter the ceremony?

Do not enter while prayers are being recited.

Will the bereaved family be present at the church or funeral home before the ceremony?

Possibly.

Is there a traditional greeting for the family?

Express your condolences.

Will there be an open casket?

Sometimes.

Is a guest expected to view the body?

This is entirely optional.

What is appropriate behavior upon viewing the body?

Pause briefly in front of the casket, then take a seat in the church sanctuary or the room in the funeral home where the service will be held.

Who are the major officiants at the ceremony and what do they do?

◼ *The pastor,* who reads from the Scriptures.
◼ *Family and/or friends,* who may deliver a eulogy.

What books are used?

Most congregations use either the New International Version or the New American Standard translations of the Bible.

To indicate the order of the ceremony:

A program will be provided and periodic announcements will also be made by the pastor.

Will a guest who is not a member of the Evangelical Free Church be expected to do anything other than sit?

Stand with the other guests. It is entirely optional for non-church members to sing and read prayers aloud with church members.

Are there any parts of the ceremony in which a guest who is not a member of the Evangelical Free Church should *not* participate?

No.

If not disruptive to the ceremony, is it okay to:

◗ **Take pictures?** No.
◗ **Use a flash?** No.
◗ **Use a video camera?** No.
◗ **Use a tape recorder?** Possibly.

Will contributions to the church be collected at the ceremony?

No.

THE INTERMENT

Should guests attend the interment?

Only if they are invited to do so. Some interments are public; some are private.

Whom should one ask for directions?

The funeral director, the ushers or family members.

What happens at the graveside?

Prayers are recited and the pastor reads from the Bible.

Do guests who are not members of the Evangelical Free Church participate at the graveside ceremony?

No. They are simply present.

COMFORTING THE BEREAVED

Is it appropriate to visit the home of the bereaved after the funeral?

Yes.

Will there be a religious service at the home of the bereaved?

No.

Will food be served?

Invariably after a funeral and the graveside service that follows, family and friends are invited back to the church for a lunch. Occasionally, the church will serve lunch to the family of the deceased and their close friends at the home of the bereaved.

How soon after the funeral will a mourner usually return to a normal work schedule?

This depends entirely on one's individual preference. The Church has no set tradition.

How soon after the funeral will a mourner usually return to a normal social schedule?

This depends entirely on one's individual preference. The Church has no set tradition.

Are there mourning customs to which a friend who is not a member of the Evangelical Free Church should be sensitive?

No. The Church has no rituals of mourning.

Are there rituals for observing the anniversary of the death?

No.

15

Greek Orthodox

HISTORY AND BELIEFS

The Orthodox Church was essentially an outgrowth of the Great Schism over doctrinal issues between east and west in the Christian world in the year 1054. This caused a complete breakdown in communication between the Roman Catholic Church, based in Rome, and the Orthodox church, which remained under the jurisdiction of the Patriarch of Constantinople (present day Istanbul).

The word "Greek" is used not just to describe the Orthodox Christian people of Greece and others who speak Greek, but to refer to the early Christians who originally formed the initial Christian church and whose members spoke Greek and used Greek thought to find appropriate expressions of the Orthodox faith.

The term "Orthodox" is used to reflect adherents' belief that they believe and worship God correctly.

Essentially, Orthodox Christians consider their beliefs similar to those of other Christian traditions, but believe that the balance and integrity of the teachings of Jesus' twelve apostles have been preserved inviolate by their church.

Greek Orthodoxy holds that the eternal truths of God's saving revelation in Jesus Christ are preserved in the living tradition of the church under the guidance and inspiration of the Holy Spirit, which is the empowering spirit of God and the particular endowment of the church. While the Bible is the written testimony of God's revelation, Holy Tradition is the all-encompassing experience of the church under the guidance and direction of the Holy Spirit.

The first Greek Orthodox community in the Americas was founded in 1864 in New Orleans by a small colony of Greek merchants. In 1892, the first permanent community of Greek Orthodox in the United States was founded in New York. This is now known as the Archdiocesan Cathedral of the Holy Trinity and See of the Archbishop of North and South America.

There are now about seven million Orthodox Christians in the Western Hemisphere.

U.S. churches: 500
U.S. membership: 1.5 million
(data from the Greek Orthodox Diocese of America)

Canadian churches: 76
Canadian membership: 350,000
(data from the 1998 Yearbook of American and Canadian Churches)

FUNERALS AND MOURNING

The Greek Orthodox Church believes that death is the separation of the soul (the spiritual dimension of each human being) from the body (the physical dimension of each human being). Upon death, we immediately begin to experience a foretaste of heaven and hell. This experience, known as the partial judgment, is based on the general character of our lives regarding behavior, character and communion with God.

At some unknown time in the future, teaches the church, Jesus Christ will return and inaugurate a new era in which His kingdom shall be established. The final judgment will then occur. In our resurrected existence, we will either live eternally in heaven in communion with God, or eternally in hell and out of communion with God.

The 30- to 60-minute Greek Orthodox funeral ceremony is not part of a larger service.

BEFORE THE CEREMONY

How soon after the death does the funeral usually take place?
Within one week; most often within two to three days.

What should a non-Greek Orthodox do upon hearing of the death of a member of that faith?
Telephone or visit the family of the deceased, or send cards and/or flowers. If visiting, one should express condolences. It is traditional for Greek

Orthodox to say to the bereaved, "May you have an abundant life" and "May their memory be eternal."

APPROPRIATE ATTIRE

Men: Jacket and tie. A headcovering is not required.

Women: A dress or a skirt and blouse or a pants suit. Neither clothing that covers the arms, hems that extend below the knees or a headcovering are required. Open-toed shoes and modest jewelry may be worn.

There are no rules regarding colors of clothing, but navy blue or black clothes are recommended for both men and women.

GIFTS

Is it appropriate to send flowers or make a contribution?
Flowers may be sent either to the home of the bereaved upon hearing the news or to the funeral itself. Contributions of $50 or more can be made to a fund or charity designated by the family of the deceased.

Is it appropriate to send food?
No. However, the family of the deceased usually provides a "mercy meal" after the funeral for relatives and friends. This may be held in a restaurant, a church hall or a private home.

THE CEREMONY

Where will the ceremony take place?
In a church.

When should guests arrive and where should they sit?
It is customary to arrive early. Ushers will advise guests where to sit.

If arriving late, are there times when a guest should *not* enter the service?
No.

Will the bereaved family be present at the church before the service?
Yes.

Is there a traditional greeting for the family?
Yes, "Memory Eternal." Or offer your condolences.

Will there be an open casket?
Usually.

Is a guest expected to view the body?
This is optional.

What is appropriate behavior upon viewing the body?
Pause briefly in front of the casket. Traditionally, when Greek Orthodox view the body, they bow in front of the casket and kiss an icon or cross placed on the chest of the deceased. Such rituals are optional for guests who are not Greek Orthodox.

Who are the major officiants at the ceremony and what do they do?
The priest, who leads the service.

What books are used?
Several books may be used, such as *The Divine Liturgy of St. John Chrysostom* (Brookline, Ma.: Holy Cross Orthodox Press, 1985).

Will a guest who is not Greek Orthodox be expected to do anything other than sit?
Yes. Stand when the congregation does and pay respects to the bereaved family.

Are there any parts of the ceremony in which a guest who is not Greek Orthodox should *not* participate?
No.

If not disruptive to the ceremony, is it okay to:
■ **Take pictures?** No.
■ **Use a flash?** No.
■ **Use a video camera?** No.
■ **Use a tape recorder?** No.

Will contributions to the church be collected at the ceremony?
No.

THE INTERMENT

Should guests attend the interment?
Yes.

Whom should one ask for directions?
The funeral director.

What happens at the graveside?

There is a five-minute prayer ceremony and each person present places one flower on the casket. The flowers usually come from those sent to the church for the funeral and then conveyed to the cemetery with the casket.

COMFORTING THE BEREAVED

Is it appropriate to visit the home of the bereaved after the funeral?

Yes, briefly.

Will there be a religious service at the home of the bereaved?

No.

Will food be served?

Yes.

How soon after the funeral will a mourner usually return to a normal work schedule?

The bereaved usually stays home from work for one week.

How soon after the funeral will a mourner usually return to a normal social schedule?

The bereaved usually avoids social gatherings for two months.

Are there mourning customs to which a friend who is not Greek Orthodox should be sensitive?

Widows may wear black for up to two years.

Are there rituals for observing the anniversary of the death?

A memorial service is held on the Sunday closest to the 40th day after the death. Subsequent memorial services are held on the annual anniversaries of the death.

16
Hindu

HISTORY AND BELIEFS

There are extraordinary differences between Hindu culture and beliefs and the prevailing Judeo-Christian religions and cultures in North America. Yet, from the Transcendentalists in New England in the early 19th century through the beatniks of the 1950s and the spiritual seekers of today, Hinduism has held a fascination for many thousands of North Americans. Most of these were either influenced tangentially by Hinduism or became actual practitioners of certain aspects of it for a while. But today, the vast majority of Hindus in the United States and Canada are immigrants from Asia, especially from India.

Unlike other religions, Hinduism has no founder and no common creed or doctrine. Generally, it teaches that God is both within being and object in the universe—and transcends every being and object; that the essence of each soul is divine; and that the purpose of life is to become aware of that divine essence. The many forms of worship ritual and meditation in Hinduism are intended to lead the soul toward direct experience of God or Self.

In general, the different gods and goddesses in Hinduism are different ways of conceiving and approaching the one God beyond name and form. Different forms of worship through images, symbols and rituals are helpful to different kinds of persons. Some do not need external worship. The goal is to transcend these forms and the world as it is ordinarily perceived and to realize the divine presence everywhere.

U.S. temples: Not available
U.S. membership: 1 million
(1995 data from The Vedanta Society)

Canadian temples: Not available
Canadian membership: 100,000+
(data from the 1992 Corpus Almanac & Canadian Sourcebook)

FUNERALS AND MOURNING

Hinduism teaches that although the physical body dies, *atman* ("AHT-mahn"), or the individual soul, has no beginning and no end. It may, upon death, pass into another reincarnation, the condition of which depends on the *karma*, or consequences of one's actions, reaped during the life that just ended, as well as during previous lifetimes.

But if, over many lifetimes, the deceased has realized the true nature of reality, the individuality of the soul will be lost upon death and it will become one with Brahman, the One, All-Encompassing soul.

BEFORE THE CEREMONY

How soon after the death does the funeral usually take place?
Usually within 24 hours.

What should a non-Hindu do upon hearing of the death of a member of that faith?
Telephone or visit the bereaved and offer your condolences.

APPROPRIATE ATTIRE

Men: Dress casually. No head covering is required.

Women: Dress casually. Not required are a head covering, clothing that covers the arms or hems that reach below the knees. Open-toed shoes and modest jewelry are permissible.

Wear white clothing. Black is not appropriate.

GIFTS

Is it appropriate to send flowers or make a contribution?
It is appropriate to personally bring flowers to the home of the deceased upon hearing of the death. In Hinduism, there is no concept of a "funeral home," so the body remains at the home until taken to the place of

cremation, which is usually 24 hours after death. Flowers are placed at the feet of the deceased.

Donations are not customary.

Is it appropriate to send food?
No.

THE CEREMONY

Where will the ceremony take place?
At the place of cremation.

When should guests arrive and where should they sit?
Arrive at the time for which the ceremony has been called. Sit wherever you wish.

If arriving late, are there times when a guest should *not* enter the ceremony?
No.

Will the bereaved family be present at the place of cremation before the ceremony?
Yes.

Is there a traditional greeting for the family?
No. Just offer your condolences.

Will there be an open casket?
Always.

Is a guest expected to view the body?
Yes.

What is appropriate behavior upon viewing the body?
Look reverently upon the body and do not touch it.

Who are the major officiants at the ceremony and what do they do?
⌐ *Priests* or senior members of the family.

What books are used?
Special books containing mantras for funeral services. Only the priests use these.

To indicate the order of the ceremony:
Ordinarily, neither a program is distributed nor are periodic announcements made by the officiating priests. The ceremony just proceeds,

although in the United States and Canada, the priest may occasionally explain the ceremony to guests who are not Hindus.

Will a guest who is not a Hindu be expected to do anything other than sit?
No.

Are there any parts of the ceremony in which a guest who is not a Hindu should *not* participate?
Guests of other faiths are welcome to participate in any aspects of the service if these do not compromise or violate their own religious beliefs.

If not disruptive to the ceremony, is it okay to:
◾ **Take pictures?** No.
◾ **Use a flash?** No.
◾ **Use a video camera?** No.
◾ **Use a tape recorder?** No.

Will contributions to the temple be collected at the ceremony?
No.

THE CREMATION

Should guests attend the cremation?
If they wish to.

Whom should one ask for directions?
Ask family members.

What happens at the cremation?
The last food offering is symbolically made to the deceased and then the body is cremated. The cremation ceremony is called *mukhagni* ("moo-KAHG-nee").

Do guests who are not Hindus participate at the cremation ceremony?
No. They are simply present.

COMFORTING THE BEREAVED

Is it appropriate to visit the home of the bereaved after the funeral?
Yes. Visit the bereaved before the *shraddha* ("SHRAHD-hah") ceremony, which occurs 10 days after the death for members of the Bhrahmin caste

and 30 days after the death for members of other castes. The ceremony is intended to liberate the soul of the deceased for its ascent to heaven. Visitors are expected to bring fruit to the home of the bereaved.

Will there be a religious service at the home of the bereaved?

The *shraddha* ceremony is performed at home. Guests are usually invited to it by phone.

Will food be served?

Varies according to tradition.

How soon after the funeral will a mourner usually return to a normal work schedule?

In 10 to 30 days, depending on when the *shraddha* ceremony is performed.

How soon after the funeral will a mourner usually return to a normal social schedule?

After the *shraddha* ceremony, which occurs 10 to 30 days after the death.

Are there mourning customs to which a friend who is not a Hindu should be sensitive?

For 10 to 30 days after the death, depending on when the *shraddha* ceremony is performed, mourners dress, eat and behave austerely.

Are there rituals for observing the anniversary of the death?

Yes. These are performed by a priest in a temple. There is no name for these rituals.

17

International Church of the Foursquare Gospel

HISTORY AND BELIEFS

The International Church of the Foursquare Gospel was founded in 1923 in Los Angeles by Aimee Semple McPherson. The new Church was an outgrowth of the revival movement in the United States that had begun at the turn of the century. Many involved in the movement spoke "in tongues" (in a language unknown to those speaking it), and claims were made of divine healing that saved lives. Since many of these experiences were associated with the coming of the Holy Spirit (the empowering quality of God) on the Day of Pentecost, participants in the revival were called Pentecostals.

"Foursquare" is a biblical term used in the Book of Exodus to refer to the tabernacle, in the Book of Ezekiel to refer to the Temple of the Lord, and in the Book of Revelation to refer to Heaven. Aimee Semple McPherson first used the term "Foursquare Gospel" during an evangelical campaign in Oakland, California, in 1922. It represents that which is equally balanced on all sides, and which is established and enduring. Such confidence in the power of the Gospel is also expressed by a New Testament verse (Hebrews 13:8) that is displayed in Foursquare churches: "Jesus Christ the Same, Yesterday, Today, and Forever."

The "Foursquare Gospel" presents Jesus Christ as Savior of the world, Baptizer with the Holy Spirit, the Great Physician, and the Soon-Coming King. It shares with the entire Pentecostal movement the concept that the truth of the Baptism is proven when the Holy Spirit empowers one to speak in tongues. The Church also shares the core Pentecostal belief in bodily healing rooted in individual atonement.

Men and women participate equally at all levels of the Church.

Official business of the International Church of the Foursquare Gospel is conducted by a president, a board of directors that is called the Foursquare Cabinet and an executive council. The Church's highest authority is its annual convention, which has the sole authority to make or amend the Church's by-laws.

District supervisors are appointed by the president, with the approval of the board of directors for districts in the United States. They are ratified by the pastors of their respective districts every four years. The ministry of each local congregation is cared for by a pastor, a church council, deacons and deaconesses and elders. Each church is expected to contribute monthly to missionary work in the United States and abroad.

In Canada, a national church, the Foursquare Gospel Church of Canada, was formed in 1981.

The Church's strong emphasis on missionary work has produced more than 80 Hispanic churches in North America and at least four major churches that minister to African-Americans. Abroad, 17,226 congregations serve 1.8 million adherents.

U.S. churches: 1,773
U.S. membership: 229,600
(*data from the* 1998 Yearbook of American and Canadian Churches)

Canadian churches: 54
Canadian membership: 3,063
(*data from the* 1998 Yearbook of American and Canadian Churches)

FUNERALS AND MOURNING

Members of the International Church of the Foursquare Gospel believe that all Christians who have died will one day rise from their graves and meet the Lord. Meanwhile, Christians who are still alive will be raptured (caught up with those who have risen from their graves) and will also be with the Lord. All who have thus joined with God will live forever.

An International Church of the Foursquare Gospel funeral usually begins with singing, Scripture reading or prayer. This is followed with hymns, prayer and worship to God and a sermon by the pastor.

A ceremony in itself, the funeral service lasts about 30 to 60 minutes.

BEFORE THE CEREMONY

How soon after the death does the funeral usually take place?

Within two to three days.

What should someone who is not a member of the International Church of the Foursquare Gospel do upon hearing of the death of a member of that faith?

Telephone or visit the bereaved to offer condolences and sympathies and offer to assist in any way possible.

APPROPRIATE ATTIRE

Men: A jacket and tie. No head covering is required.

Women: A dress or a skirt and blouse. Clothing need not cover the arms and hems need not reach below the knees. Open-toed shoes and modest jewelry are permissible. No head covering is required.

Dark, somber colors for clothing are advised.

GIFTS

Is it appropriate to send flowers or make a contribution?

Flowers may be sent to the funeral home or church where the funeral service is held. Contributions may be sent to a memorial fund determined by the bereaved.

Is it appropriate to send food?

Yes. Send it to the home of the bereaved.

THE CEREMONY

Where will the ceremony take place?

At a funeral home.

When should guests arrive and where should they sit?

Arrive at the time for which the ceremony has been scheduled. Ushers usually advise guests where to sit.

If arriving late, are there times when a guest should *not* enter the ceremony?

No.

Will the bereaved family be present at the funeral home before the ceremony?

Possibly.

Is there a traditional greeting for the family?

Just offer your condolences.

Will there be an open casket?

Usually.

Is a guest expected to view the body?

This is optional.

What is appropriate behavior upon viewing the body?

Look into the casket while walking slowly past it, then take a seat in the room in the funeral parlor where the service will be held.

Who are the major officiants at the ceremony and what do they do?

▪ *The pastor,* who delivers a sermon.

What books are used?

None.

To indicate the order of the ceremony:

A program will be distributed and a display will indicate the order of prayers and hymns.

Will a guest who is not a member of the International Church of the Foursquare Gospel be expected to do anything other than sit?

Yes. It is expected for guests to stand with the congregants. If it does not violate their religious beliefs, it is entirely optional for guests to sing with the congregants and to pray aloud with them.

Are there any parts of the ceremony in which a guest who is not a member of the International Church of the Foursquare Gospel should *not* participate?

No.

If not disruptive to the ceremony, is it okay to:

▪ **Take pictures?** No.
▪ **Use a flash?** No.

▪ **Use a video camera?** No.
▪ **Use a tape recorder?** Yes.

Will contributions to the church be collected at the ceremony?
No.

THE INTERMENT

Should guests attend the interment?

Attendance is optional.

Whom should one ask for directions?

An usher or the funeral director or just follow the funeral procession.

What happens at the graveside?

There are prayers, songs and Scripture readings, and the casket is buried.

Do guests who are not members of the International Church of the Foursquare Gospel participate at the graveside ceremony?

No, they are simply present.

COMFORTING THE BEREAVED

Is it appropriate to visit the home of the bereaved after the funeral?

Yes, if one knows the family well. Visit briefly.

Will there be a religious service at the home of the bereaved?
No.

Will food be served?

Possibly, but not alcoholic beverages.

How soon after the funeral will a mourner usually return to a normal work schedule?

Two days to a week, depending upon the mourner's relationship to the deceased and individual preference. The Church has no set tradition.

How soon after the funeral will a mourner usually return to a normal social schedule?

This is entirely the choice of the bereaved, since the Church has no set tradition. It may be one or two weeks or more, and is often primarily determined by local cultural traditions and one's relationship to the deceased.

Are there mourning customs to which a friend who is not a member of the International Church of the Foursquare Gospel should be sensitive?

No.

Are there rituals for observing the anniversary of the death?

No.

18

International
Pentecostal Holiness Church

HISTORY AND BELIEFS

The International Pentecostal Holiness Church has its origins in the first Pentecostal denominations in the United States: The Pentecostal Holiness Church, the Fire-Baptized Holiness Church, and the Tabernacle Pentecostal Church. The first two churches merged in 1911; the last church joined them in 1915. In Canada, it is known as the Pentecostal Holiness Church of Canada.

The church emphasizes direct access to God, the Father; believes prayer can manifest miracles, especially divine healing; and is certain that the Holy Spirit may be evidenced during worship services by certain congregants speaking "in tongues," which are languages unknown to the speaker. The church also teaches the imminent coming of Jesus Christ and that Jesus shed His blood for the complete cleansing of those who believe in Him from all indwelling sin.

Worldwide, the 12,802 churches of the International Pentecostal Holiness Church have 2.3 million members. The Church also has 155 missionaries in 80 countries.

The government of the Church gives individual churches a measure of denominational uniformity and local autonomy.

U.S. churches: 1,653
U.S. membership: 157,163
(*data from the* 1998 Yearbook of American and Canadian Churches)

Canadian churches: Not available
Canadian membership: 2,500
(data from the Pentecostal Holiness Church of Canada)

FUNERALS AND MOURNING

Members of the International Pentecostal Holiness Church believe that all Christians who have died will one day rise from their graves and meet the Lord in the air. Meanwhile, Christians who are still alive will be raptured (or caught up with those who have risen from their graves) and will also be with the Lord. All who have thus joined with God will live forever.

A funeral usually includes singing, Scripture reading or prayer. This is followed with hymns, prayer and worship to God, and a sermon by the pastor.

A ceremony in itself, the funeral service lasts about 30 to 60 minutes.

BEFORE THE CEREMONY

How soon after the death does the funeral usually take place?

Within two to three days.

What should someone who is not a member of the International Pentecostal Holiness Church do upon hearing of the death of a member of that faith?

Telephone, visit or write the bereaved to offer condolences and sympathies and offer to assist in any way possible.

APPROPRIATE ATTIRE

Men: A jacket and tie. No head covering is required.

Women: A dress or a skirt and blouse. Shorts, halters, jeans, T-shirts and revealing attire are never appropriate. Clothing need not cover the arms and hems need not reach below the knees. Open-toed shoes and modest jewelry are permissible. No head covering is required.

Dark, somber colors for clothing are advised.

GIFTS

Is it appropriate to send flowers or make a contribution?

Flowers may be sent to the funeral home or the church where the funeral service is held. Contributions may be sent to a memorial fund determined by the bereaved.

Is it appropriate to send food?

Yes. Send any food you deem appropriate to the home of the bereaved.

THE CEREMONY

Where will the ceremony take place?

Either in a church or a funeral home.

When should guests arrive and where should they sit?

Arrive at the time for which the ceremony has been scheduled. Ushers usually advise guests where to sit.

If arriving late, are there times when a guest should *not* enter the ceremony?

No.

Will the bereaved family be present at the church or funeral home before the ceremony?

Yes.

Is there a traditional greeting for the family?

Just offer your condolences.

Will there be an open casket?

Usually.

Is a guest expected to view the body?

This is optional.

What is appropriate behavior upon viewing the body?

Look into the casket while walking slowly past it, then take a seat in the church sanctuary or the room in the funeral parlor where the service will be held.

Who are the major officiants at the ceremony and what do they do?

- *The minister,* who delivers a brief sermon and tribute to the deceased.
- *Family members and close friends,* who deliver eulogies.
- *Musicians,* who sing one or two songs.

What books are used?

The Bible and sometimes a hymnal. The most common versions of the Bible used in the Church are the Authorized King James Version, the New King James Version, the New International Version and the New American Standard Version. A variety of hymnals are used.

To indicate the order of the ceremony:

A program is sometimes distributed.

Will a guest who is not a member of the International Pentecostal Holiness Church be expected to do anything other than sit?

No. It is entirely optional for guests of other faiths to stand and sing with congregants.

Are there any parts of the ceremony in which a guest who is not a member of the International Pentecostal Holiness Church should *not* participate?

No.

If not disruptive to the ceremony, is it okay to:

▪ **Take pictures?** Yes.
▪ **Use a flash?** Yes.
▪ **Use a video camera?** Yes.
▪ **Use a tape recorder?** Yes.

Will contributions to the church be collected at the ceremony?

No.

THE INTERMENT

Should guests attend the interment?

Attendance is optional.

Whom should one ask for directions?

The minister or funeral director.

What happens at the graveside?

There are prayers, songs and Scripture readings, and comments about the deceased may be made by the minister, family or close friends.

Do guests who are not members of International Pentecostal Holiness Church participate at the graveside ceremony?

No, they are simply present.

COMFORTING THE BEREAVED

Is it appropriate to visit the home of the bereaved after the funeral?

Yes, if one knows the family well. It is best to limit the visit to about 15 minutes.

Will there be a religious service at the home of the bereaved?

No.

Will food be served?

Possibly, but no alcoholic beverages.

How soon after the funeral will a mourner usually return to a normal work schedule?

A week or two, depending upon individual preference. The Church has no set tradition.

How soon after the funeral will a mourner usually return to a normal social schedule?

This is entirely the choice of the bereaved, since the Church has no set tradition. It may be one or two weeks or more, and is often primarily determined by local cultural traditions.

Are there mourning customs to which a friend who is not a member of the International Pentecostal Holiness Church should be sensitive?

No.

Are there rituals for observing the anniversary of the death?

No.

19

Islam

HISTORY AND BELIEFS

The Arabic word *Islam* means "submission," and Islam is the religion of submission to the will of God ("Allah" in Arabic).

Muhammad, who is regarded as the last and final prophet of Allah, was born in Mecca (in present-day Saudi Arabia) in approximately 570 A.D. As a young man, he sought solitude in a cave on the outskirts of Mecca, where, according to Muslim belief, he received revelation from God. The basic creed that Muhammad taught is that the one God in heaven demands morality and monotheistic devotion from those He has created.

Initially, Muhammad's message was widely rejected, especially by Mecca's elite, which felt threatened by its egalitarian teachings. But by the time he died in 632 A.D., most of Arabia had embraced Islam.

Muslims revere the Qur'an, their holy book, as the earthly cornerstone of their faith.

Islam teaches that the Hebrew Bible and the New Testament were also authentic revelations from God and recognizes as prophets all those mentioned as such in those scriptures, including Abraham, Moses, David and Jesus.

With about one billion Muslims around the globe, Islam is the fastest growing religion in the world. Every country in the world has at least a small Muslim community. There are now Muslims in nearly every town in the United States, with more substantial numbers in larger cities, especially in the East and Midwest and on the West Coast. In Canada, there are Muslims in every major city, with substantial numbers in the provinces of Ontario, Alberta and British Columbia.

U.S. mosques: 1,000
U.S. membership: 6 million
(1995 data from the American Muslim Council)

Canadian Islamic Centers and Organizations: 150
Canadian membership: 450,000
(1996 data from the Muslim World League)

FUNERALS AND MOURNING

The Muslim view of the afterlife includes a universal belief in a final Day of Reckoning, when all people will be called upon to give account for their actions. The Qur'an describes the pleasures of heaven enjoyed by the righteous—as well as the torments of hell—in vivid, physical detail. Individual Muslims hold a range of differing opinions about how literally those descriptions are to be taken.

An Islamic funeral is a service in itself and usually lasts about 30 to 60 minutes. In some cases, it may last more than an hour.

BEFORE THE CEREMONY

How soon after the death does the funeral usually take place?
Two to three days.

What should a non-Muslim do upon hearing of the death of a member of that faith?
Call or visit the bereaved. If one visits, shake hands or hug and kiss the family members of the same gender, sit and talk quietly and offer some quiet prayer.

APPROPRIATE ATTIRE

Men: Casual shirt and slacks. Head covering is not required.

Women: A dress is recommended. Clothing should cover the arms and hems should reach below the knees. A scarf is required to cover the head.

For both men and women, there are no rules regarding colors of clothing, but openly wearing crosses, Stars of David, jewelry with the signs of the zodiac and pendants with faces or heads of animals or people is discouraged.

Dark, somber colors are advised.

GIFTS

Is it appropriate to send flowers or make a contribution?
Send flowers after the funeral to the home of the bereaved.

Is it appropriate to send food?
Yes.

THE CEREMONY

Where will the ceremony take place?
At a funeral home or in the general purpose room of the mosque.

When should guests arrive and where should they sit?
Arrive at the time set for the funeral. An usher will advise guests on where to sit.

If arriving late, are there times when a guest should *not* enter the ceremony?
No.

Will the bereaved family be present at the funeral home before the ceremony?
No.

Is there a traditional greeting for the family?
No. Just offer your condolences.

Will there be an open casket?
Never.

Who are the major officiants at the ceremony and what do they do?
◼ *An imam*, who presides.

What books are used?
The Qur'an.

To indicate the order of the ceremony:
No directions are given during the service, which is intended to be as simple as possible.

Will a guest who is not a Muslim be expected to do anything other than sit?
No.

Are there any parts of the ceremony in which a guest who is not a Muslim should *not* participate?
No.

If not disruptive to the ceremony, is it okay to:
◧ **Take pictures?** No.
◧ **Use a flash?** No.
◧ **Use a video camera?** No.
◧ **Use a tape recorder?** No.

Will contributions to the mosque be collected at the ceremony?
No.

THE INTERMENT

Should guests attend the interment?
Yes.

Whom should one ask for directions?
An imam.

What happens at the graveside?
The *Janazah* prayers ("jah-NAH-zah") for the dead are recited and the deceased is buried. Muslims are never cremated.

Do guests who are not Muslims participate at the graveside ceremony?
No, they are simply present.

COMFORTING THE BEREAVED

Is it appropriate to visit the home of the bereaved after the funeral?
Yes. Visit any time during the days of mourning, which are religiously mandated not to exceed 40 days. The number of mourning days that one actually observes is individually set and can be determined by telephoning the home of the bereaved. When visiting the home of a mourner, talk quietly with the bereaved and other visitors. Often, visitors and mourners sit in silence while someone reads aloud from the Qur'an or a tape of a reading from the Qur'an is played.

Will there be a religious service at the home of the bereaved?
No.

Will food be served?

Possibly. Often, women in the local Muslim community prepare food for mourners and their guests.

How soon after the funeral will a mourner usually return to a normal work schedule?

Usually after a few days.

How soon after the funeral will a mourner usually return to a normal social schedule?

There are no prescriptions in Islam about such matters. This is more culturally determined than religiously determined. Usually, women do not engage in normal social activities until 40 days after the death of a member of their immediate family. There are no norms for men.

Are there mourning customs to which a friend who is not a Muslim should be sensitive?

The bereaved usually wear black, although this is a cultural norm and not a religious prescription.

Are there rituals for observing the anniversary of the death?

No.

20

Jehovah's Witnesses

HISTORY AND BELIEFS

The Jehovah's Witnesses are a worldwide faith known for their assertive proselytizing and their expectations of an imminent apocalypse. They have drawn attention because of their refusal to celebrate Christmas, by their dedicated missionary work and by using Jehovah as the sole name of God.

Jehovah's Witnesses derive their name from the 43rd chapter of the Book of Isaiah, in which the gods of the nations are invited to bring forth their witnesses to prove their claimed cases of righteousness or to hear the witnesses for Jehovah's side and acknowledge the truth: "Ye are My witnesses, saith Jehovah, and My servants whom I have chosen; that ye may know and believe Me, and understand that I am He; before Me there was no God formed, neither shall there be after Me. I, even I, am Jehovah; and besides Me there is no savior" (Isaiah 43:10, 11, American Standard Version of the Bible).

In the Bible, all faithful worshippers, such as Abel, Noah, Abraham and Jesus, were called "witnesses of God" (Hebrews 11:1-12:1; Revelation 3:14).

The faith was founded in western Pennsylvania in the early 1870s by Charles Taze Russell, who had organized a Bible study group to promote the basic teachings of the Bible. It was his desire to return to the teachings of first-century Christianity.

Jehovah's Witnesses believe that God demands unconditional obedience and that the infallible source of truth is the Bible, which is true in every detail. Jesus, who was the Son of God and was His first creation, was responsible for all the rest of God's creation on earth. While residing on earth, Jesus was entirely a man. After His death, He was raised by God to heaven and restored to a place second only to that of His Father, Jehovah.

The fulfillment of God's kingdom will occur through the battle of Armageddon, the appearance of the Lord in the air, the thousand-year rule on earth of Christ (during which resurrection and judgment take place). This process began in 1914 and its completion will soon occur.

Members of the Church are expected to devote their primary loyalty and time to the movement, and not participate in politics or interfaith movements. They believe that all human laws that do not conflict with God's law should be obeyed. They also do not vote in civic elections or serve in the military. They respect each country's flag (or other national symbols), but do not salute it, since they believe this would be idolatry.

U.S. churches: 11,000
U.S. membership: 985,000
(data from the 1998 Yearbook of Jehovah's Witnesses*)*

Canadian churches: 1,400
Canadian membership: 114,000
(data from the 1998 Yearbook of Jehovah's Witnesses*)*

FUNERALS AND MOURNING

Jehovah's Witnesses believe that the dead are "conscious of nothing at all" and are asleep in the grave awaiting resurrection to life. While the majority will be raised to life in an earthly paradise, a small number—144,000—will be raised as immortal spirit creatures to rule with Christ in the heavenly Kingdom of God.

The funeral service, which is a ceremony in itself, may last about 15 to 30 minutes.

BEFORE THE CEREMONY

How soon after the death does the funeral usually take place?
Usually within one week.

What should a non-Jehovah's Witness do upon hearing of the death of a member of that faith?
Telephone or visit the bereaved to offer your condolences.

APPROPRIATE ATTIRE

Men: A jacket and tie. No head covering is required.

Women: A dress or a skirt and blouse. Dress "modestly" and "sensibly." Hems need not reach below the knees nor must clothing cover the arms. Open-toed shoes and modest jewelry are permissible. No head covering is required.

There are no rules regarding colors of clothing, but what is worn should respect the somberness of the occasion.

GIFTS

Is it appropriate to send flowers or make a contribution?
Yes. Flowers may be sent to the home of the bereaved before or after the funeral or to the funeral home. Notice that contributions in memory of the deceased have been donated to a charity can be sent to the mourners' home before or after the funeral.

Is it appropriate to send food?
Yes. This can be sent to the home of the bereaved before or after the funeral.

THE CEREMONY

Where will the ceremony take place?
Either at a Kingdom Hall or in a funeral home.

When should guests arrive and where should they sit?
Arrive early to avoid causing a distraction. Attendants will seat guests. The front few rows are reserved for family.

If arriving late, are there times when a guest should *not* enter the ceremony?
No, but attendants will direct latecomers to seats.

Will the bereaved family be present at the Kingdom Hall or funeral home before the ceremony?
Possibly.

Is there a traditional greeting for the family?
No. Just offer your condolences.

Will there be an open casket?
Possibly. This depends on the preference of the immediate family.

Is a guest expected to view the body?
There are no such expectations.

What is appropriate behavior upon viewing the body?
Look upon it somberly for a few moments.

Who are the major officiants at the ceremony and what do they do?
◾ *The Congregation Elder,* who will deliver a talk from the Bible designed to comfort the bereaved.

What books are used?
Usually no books are used by the audience. Occasionally, a Bible, such as the New World Translation (New York: The Watchtower Bible and Tract Society of New York, 1961) or a songbook, such as *Sing Praises to Jehovah* (New York: The Watchtower Bible and Tract Society of New York, 1984) may be used.

To indicate the order of the ceremony:
Directions are not necessary because of the brevity of the service, which is led entirely by the Congregation Elder.

Will a guest who is not a Jehovah's Witness be expected to do anything other than sit?
No.

Are there any parts of the ceremony in which a guest who is not a Jehovah's Witness should *not* participate?
No.

If not disruptive to the ceremony, is it okay to:
◾ **Take pictures?** No.
◾ **Use a flash?** No.
◾ **Use a video camera?** No.
◾ **Use a tape recorder?** Yes.

Will contributions to the church be collected at the ceremony?
No.

THE INTERMENT

Should guests attend the interment?
Such attendance is done at the discretion of the guest.

Whom should one ask for directions?
The funeral director or his or her assistants.

What happens at the graveside?
Brief comments on the Scriptures are followed by prayer.

Do guests who are not Jehovah's Witnesses participate at the graveside ceremony?
No, they are simply present.

COMFORTING THE BEREAVED

Is it appropriate to visit the home of the bereaved after the funeral?
Yes. The length of the visit depends on the circumstances. Discussing with the bereaved what you appreciated about the deceased is helpful.

Will there be a religious service at the home of the bereaved?
No.

Will food be served?
Possibly. This depends on the preference of the mourners.

How soon after the funeral will a mourner usually return to a normal work schedule?
This depends on the preferences and the circumstances of the mourners. There is no set time for remaining away from work, although mourners are usually absent from work for at least a few days.

How soon after the funeral will a mourner usually return to a normal social schedule?
This is entirely an individual matter and depends on the preferences and the circumstances of the mourners. There is no set time for abstaining from social activities.

Are there mourning customs to which a friend who is not a Jehovah's Witness should be sensitive?
No.

Are there rituals for observing the anniversary of the death?
No.

21

Jewish

HISTORY AND BELIEFS

Judaism includes religious rituals and beliefs along with a code of ethical behavior. It also incorporates and reflects the ancient history of the Jews as a nation in its rituals, ceremonies and celebrations. Today, its adherents include people of every race and most nations.

The foundation of Judaism is the Torah, the first five books of the Bible (Genesis, Exodus, Leviticus, Numbers and Deuteronomy). According to the Torah, God made a covenant with the Jews, beginning with the three patriarchs: Abraham; his son, Isaac; and his grandson, Jacob, whose name God changed to "Israel." At a time when people worshipped many gods, the Jewish people, through this covenant, accepted the "One God" as the only God.

Central to this covenant is the concept of being "chosen" as a people, for as Moses tells his people in the Bible: "...The Lord has chosen you to be a people for His own possession, out of all the peoples that are on the face of the earth" (Deuteronomy 14:2). Being "chosen" does not confer special privilege. It means that the Jewish poeple are obliged to bring God's message to the world.

As part of God's covenant with Abraham, his descendants were promised the area now known as Israel—the Promised Land—as their homeland. They took possession of it in approximately 1200 B.C.E. (Before the Common Era, referred to as B.C. in the Christian calendar). In 70 C.E. (Common Era, referred to as A.D. in the Christian calendar), the conquering Romans destroyed Jerusalem and its Temple, which was the center of Jewish religious life, and drove the Jewish people from their land to end repeated rebellions. This began the period known as "The Diaspora," when the Jewish people were without a homeland. Many drifted to the northern and southern rim of the Mediterranean, while others emigrated eastward.

Jewish settlement in the American colonies began in 1654 in New Amsterdam (later called New York). Jewish immigration to Canada began in 1760, with the first synagogue being established in 1768. The modern Jewish state, Israel, was founded in 1948, three years after the end of the Holocaust in which six million Jews were killed.

Before the Diaspora, Judaism as a religion evolved under a hereditary priesthood that officiated at the Temple in Jerusalem, and through the ethical and moral teachings of a series of prophets. Following the Temple's destruction, religious leadership passed from priests to *rabbis*—teachers and scholars. Today, the rabbinate includes both men and women in all movements except the Orthodox.

There are now four major Jewish religious movements in the United States and Canada. In terms of theology, Reform Judaism is at the liberal end followed by Reconstructionist, Conservative, and Orthodox—both modern and traditional (which includes several fundamentalist groups, such as the Hasidim).

Hebrew, the traditional language of Jewish worship, is used to varying degrees in the services or celebrations of each movement. Each also has its own version of the prayerbook, and almost all include translations of the Hebrew material.

Reform Judaism, which began in the early 19th century in Germany, regards Judaism as an ongoing process resulting from the relationship between God and the Jewish people over its history. It considers Torah divinely inspired and subject to individual interpretation based on study, and emphasizes the ethical and moral messages of the prophets to help create a just society.

Reconstructionism, founded in the 1930s, is the most recent of the Jewish movements. Here the essence of Judaism is defined as embodying an entire civilization and not only a religion. At the core of this civilization is a people who have the authority and the responsibility to "reconstruct" its contents from generation to generation.

Conservative Judaism began in the mid-19th century as a reaction to what its founders perceived to be Reform's radicalism. It teaches that while the Torah as a whole is binding and that much of Jewish law remains authoritative, nonetheless new ideas and practices have always influenced Jewish beliefs and rituals and this should continue today, as well.

Orthodox Judaism teaches that Torah was divinely revealed to Moses at Mount Sinai and that the *halachah* ("hah-lah-KHAH"), the interpretative process of that law, is both divinely guided and authoritative. Thus, no law stemming from the Torah can be tampered with even if it displeases modern sensibilities. Orthodoxy often rejects more modern forms of Judaism as deviations from divine truths and authentic modes of Jewish life.

Houses of worship in the Orthodox, Conservative and Reconstructionist movement are typically called "synagogues." Usually, only a Reform house of worship is called a "temple."

U.S. synagogues/temples: Over 2,000 total
Reform: 890
Conservative: 800
Reconstructionist: 80
Orthodox: Not available

U.S. membership: 4.1 million total
Reform: 2 million
Conservative: 1.6 million
Reconstructionist: 100,000
Orthodox: 375,000 (estimate)
(1995 data from each denomination's central office, except Orthodox)

Canadian synagogues/temples: Over 248 total
Reform: 20
Conservative: 48
Reconstructionist: 2
Orthodox: 124

Canadian membership: Over 365,000 total
Reform: Not available
Conservative: Not available
Reconstructionist: Not available
Orthodox: Not available
(data from the Canadian Jewish Congress and the
1992 Corpus Almanac and Canadian Sourcebook)

FUNERALS AND MOURNING

A Jewish funeral will last between 15 and 60 minutes. It is a time of intense mourning and public grieving. It is a service in itself and is not part of a larger service.

The Reform movement rejects all notions of bodily resurrection and of a physical life after death. Instead, it believes in the immortality of every soul, which will eventually return to God. True immortality resides in memories treasured in this world by those who knew and loved the deceased.

The Reconstructionist movement does not believe in bodily resurrection. It believes that, upon death, the soul rejoins the universe.

The Conservative movement talks about the resurrection of the dead, but does not specify whether this will be a physical or a spiritual resurrection. The former would occur upon the coming of the Messiah; the latter would occur by those remaining on earth sensing and remembering the deceased.

Orthodox Jews believe in bodily resurrection and a physical life after death. This would occur upon the coming of the Messiah. In the meantime, there are rough equivalents to heaven and hell, with righteous souls enjoying the pleasures of *olam ha'bah* ("oh-LAHM hah-BAH"), "the world to come," which has a Garden of Eden-like quality; and the wicked suffering in the fiery pits of *Gehenna* ("geh-HEN-ah").

Traditional Jewish law forbids cremation, but cremation is allowed among Reform Jews.

BEFORE THE CEREMONY

How soon after the death does the funeral usually take place?

The day after the death, unless there are extraordinary circumstances. In some Reform families, within two to three days after the death.

What should a non-Jew do upon hearing of the death of a member of that faith?

Telephone or visit the bereaved at home and offer condolences and to help out in any way. Possibly bring food to their home. Especially for Orthodox families, make certain the food is kosher (conforms with traditional Jewish dietary laws). If particularly close with the bereaved, offer to take them to the funeral home to arrange details for the funeral.

APPROPRIATE ATTIRE

Men: A jacket and tie. A small headcovering called a *yarmulke* ("YAHR-mil-kah") or *kippah* ("keep-AH") is required at Orthodox, Conservative and Reconstructionist funerals and at some Reform funerals. They will be available at the funeral home or synagogue/temple.

Women: A dress or a skirt and blouse. Clothing should be modest.

At some Conservative funerals, a hat or another form of headcovering may be required. Open-toed shoes and modest jewelry are appropriate. For Orthodox funerals, clothing should cover the arms, hems should reach below the knees and heads should be covered with a hat or veil.

Do not openly wear symbols of other faiths, such as a cross.

Somber colors for clothing are recommended.

GIFTS

Is it appropriate to send flowers or make a contribution?

Flowers are never appropriate for Orthodox, Conservative and Reconstructionist funerals, but are sometimes appropriate for Reform funerals. Contributions in memory of the deceased are customary. Small contributions are often given to a charity or cause favored by the deceased and which may be listed in an obituary in a local newspaper; to a special fund established by the bereaved family; or to a Jewish organization, particularly the Jewish National Fund (42 East 69th Street, New York, N.Y. 10021; telephone (800) 345-8565) that plants trees in Israel and which will send the bereaved family a letter informing them that you have "planted a tree in Israel" in memory of the deceased.

Is it appropriate to send food?

Yes, to the home of the bereaved after the funeral. Even if the family is not ritually observant, it is best if the food is kosher (conforms with traditional Jewish dietary laws) to avoid even the possibility of offending them.

THE CEREMONY

Where will the ceremony take place?

Either at a synagogue/temple or a funeral home.

When should guests arrive and where should they sit?

Arrive on time. Ushers may be available to direct guests to seating.

If arriving late, are there times when a guest should *not* enter the ceremony?

Do not enter during the processional or recessional, if they take place, or while eulogies are being delivered.

Will the bereaved family be present at the synagogue/temple or the funeral home before the ceremony?

Yes, usually for no longer than one hour.

Is there a traditional greeting for the family?

Offer condolences, such as "I'm sorry for your loss."

Will there be an open casket?

Never.

Who are the major officiants at the ceremony and what do they do?

- *A rabbi,* who officiates and delivers a eulogy.
- *A cantor,* who sings.
- *Family member(s) or friend(s),* who may also deliver a eulogy or memorial.

What books are used?

None. The service is led entirely by the rabbi, with no lay participation other than eulogies or memorials by relative(s) or friend(s).

To indicate the order of the ceremony:

The officiating rabbi will make occasional announcements.

Will a guest who is not Jewish be expected to do anything other than sit?

Guests are expected to stand with the other mourners.

Are there any parts of the ceremony in which a guest who is not Jewish should *not* participate?

No.

If not disruptive to the ceremony, is it okay to:

- **Take pictures?** No.
- **Use a flash?** No.
- **Use a video camera?** No.
- **Use a tape recorder?** Possibly. Ask permission from a member of the deceased's immediate family.

Will contributions to the synagogue/temple be collected at the ceremony?

No.

THE INTERMENT

Should guests attend the interment?

It is expected only of family and close friends, not acquaintances.

Whom should one ask for directions?

The funeral director.

What happens at the graveside?

The service will vary, depending as much on the family's background as on its religious affiliation. At the simplest graveside service, the rabbi recites prayers and leads the family in the mourner's *kaddish* ("KAH-dish"), the prayer for the deceased. At a traditional service, once the mourners have arrived at the cemetery, there is a slow procession to the grave itself, with several pauses along the way. After prayers and *kaddish* have been recited, all present participate in filling in the grave by each putting one spadeful of earth into it. As the closest family members leave the gravesite, they pass between two rows of relatives and friends.

Do guests who are not Jews participate at the graveside ceremony?

They participate in filling in the grave, if this custom is followed. Otherwise, they are simply present.

COMFORTING THE BEREAVED

Is it appropriate to visit the home of the bereaved after the funeral?

Yes. The family sits in mourning for seven days after the funeral. This is called the *shiva* period ("SHIH-vah"). Visits should last about 30 minutes. They are usually made during the daytime or early evening hours. After expressing your condolences, it is customary to sit quietly or talk to other callers, and wait to be spoken to by the principal mourners.

There are no ritual objects at the home of the bereaved, but some home traditions during the mourning period may include:

- Covering mirrors in the home to concentrate on mourning and not on vanity.
- Burning a special memorial candle for seven days in memory of the deceased.
- Immediate members of the family sitting on small chairs or boxes; wearing a black ribbon that has been cut and slippers or just socks rather than shoes; and, for men, not shaving.

All these symbolize mourners' lack of interest in their comfort or how they appear to others.

Will there be a religious service at the home of the bereaved?

Yes. Twice a day, morning and evening. These usually last about 10 to 20 minutes. Non-Jews should take a prayerbook when these are offered and may silently read the English, if this does not violate their religious beliefs. They should stand when those present stand during the brief service.

Will food be served?

Probably. Guests should not wait for a grace or benediction before eating. Guests will eat as they arrive, after expressing their condolences to the breaved.

How soon after the funeral will a mourner usually return to a normal work schedule?

One week.

How soon after the funeral will a mourner usually return to a normal social schedule?

One month to one year, depending on the deceased's relation to the person as well as personal inclination.

Are there mourning customs to which a friend who is not Jewish should be sensitive?

For eleven months after the death of their parent or child, 30 days for other relatives, mourners who follow traditional practice will attend daily morning and/or evening services at synagogue/temple, where he (or she, too, in a more "modern" Orthodox household) participates in the service and, in particular, recites the mourners' *kaddish* ("KAH-dish"), the special prayer for the deceased.

Are there rituals for observing the anniversary of the death?

The anniversary of the death is called a *yahrzeit* ("YAHR-tzite"), upon which the bereaved attends service at a synagogue/temple and lights at home a *yahrzeit* candle that burns for 24 hours. An "unveiling" of the tombstone usually takes place on approximately the first anniversary of the death and involves a simple ceremony at the gravesite. Attendance is by specific invitation only.

22

Lutheran

HISTORY AND BELIEFS

Lutherans trace their faith back to the German reformer, Martin Luther (1483-1546), who sought to reform doctrines and practices of the Roman Catholic Church. Objecting to the Church's teachings that one is saved by faith and by doing good works, he maintained that, according to the Bible, one is made just in God's eyes only by trusting in Jesus' accomplishments for humanity. This is distinct from any good that one does.

Luther also objected to corruption among the clergy and advocated worship in the language of the people rather than in Latin. He favored a married, rather than a celibate, clergy.

Although the Church of Rome considered Luther disloyal and drove him out, later, many priests and laity, especially in northern Germany, eventually agreed with Luther's teachings and revamped already existing churches around them.

German and Scandinavian immigrants brought the Lutheran faith to North America. By 1900, scores of small Lutheran church bodies were divided from one another by language, theology and the extent of their assimilation into North American society. Although still somewhat divided along ethnic lines, the main divisions today are between those who are theologically liberal and theologically conservative.

In the United States, the two main Lutheran denominations are the Evangelical Lutheran Church in America and the Lutheran Church—Missouri Synod. The former was created by uniting many earlier churches; the latter, which is a national Church despite its name, is more conservative theologically.

In Canada, the Evangelical Lutheran Church in Canada is comparable to the Evangelical Lutheran Church in America; while the Lutheran Church–Canada, is the Canadian counterpart to the Lutheran Church–Missouri Synod, and relates closely to that body.

The Evangelical Lutheran Church in America:
U.S. churches: 11,000
U.S. membership: 5.2 million

The Lutheran Church–Missouri Synod:
U.S. churches: 6,100
U.S. membership: 2.6 million
(data from the 1998 Yearbook of American and Canadian Churches*)*

The Evangelical Lutheran Church in Canada:
Canadian churches: 864
Canadian membership: 198,683

Lutheran Church–Canada:
Canadian churches: 387
Canadian membership: 84,763
(data from Directory, Lutheran Churches in Canada, *1997)*

FUNERALS AND MOURNING

For Lutherans, death is not the end of life, but the beginning of new life. While Lutherans will grieve, they do not mourn as do those who have no hope of ever seeing the deceased again or without the sure hope that those who die in faith in Jesus Christ are assured eternal life with God.

The funeral is usually a service in itself. The pastor presides. Pall bearers carry or push the casket on rollers into the funeral home or church sanctuary. The service will rarely last more than 30 minutes. All attending are expected to remain to the end.

BEFORE THE CEREMONY

How soon after the death does the funeral usually take place?
There is no set period by which the funeral should occur, but it usually takes place within three days after death.

What should a non-Lutheran do upon hearing of the death of a member of that faith?
Call the bereaved, visit or send a note to express your sympathy at their loss. Express your care and love for the bereaved.

APPROPRIATE ATTIRE

Men: Jacket and tie. No head covering is required.

Women: A dress or skirt and blouse are acceptable. Open-toed shoes and modest jewelry are fine. Hems need not reach the knees. No head covering is required.

Local social customs govern, but conservative clothing and dark, somber colors are recommended.

GIFTS

Is it appropriate to send flowers or make a contribution?
It is appropriate to send flowers unless the family expresses otherwise. Send them to the deceased's home or to the funeral home where the funeral will be held.

It is also appropriate to make a donation in the form of a "memorial" in memory of the deceased. The family will often announce, either through the funeral home or in the funeral worship folder, the preferred charity or church for memorial contributions. Memorials are often mailed or hand-delivered to the funeral home or church office. There is no standard amount to be donated.

Is it appropriate to send food?
You may want to send food to the home of the bereaved for the family and their guests.

THE CEREMONY

Where will the ceremony take place?
Typically, in the church of the deceased, although it may be at a funeral home.

When should guests arrive and where should they sit?
It is customary to arrive early enough to be seated when the service begins. Someone will tell you where and when to sit.

If arriving late, are there times when a guest should *not* enter the ceremony?
Do not enter during the procession or prayer.

Will the bereaved family be present at the church or funeral home before the ceremony?
If there is a visitation at the funeral home the night before the funeral, you can attend and express your sorrow and regret.

Is there a traditional greeting for the family?
Just offer your condolences.

Will there be an open casket?
Possibly.

Is a guest expected to view the body?
This is optional.

What is appropriate behavior upon viewing the body?
Stand quietly and then move on.

Who are the major officiants at the ceremony and what do they do?
◪ *The pastor*, who presides.

What books are used?
A hymnal, usually the *Lutheran Book of Worship* (Minneapolis, Minn.: Augsburg Fortress, 1978) or *The Lutheran Hymnal* (St. Louis, Mo.: Concordia Publishing House, 1941) and/or *Lutheran Worship* (St. Louis, Mo.: Concordia Publishing House, 1982).

To indicate the order of the ceremony:
There will be a program or the pastor will make periodic announcements.

Will a guest who is not a Lutheran be expected to do anything other than sit?
The level of participation depends on whether or not the guest is Christian. Christians will generally be expected to stand, kneel and sing with the congregation and read prayers aloud. Non-Christians are expected to stand with congregants, but not necessarily to kneel, sing or pray with them. Remaining seated when others are kneeling is fine.

Are there any parts of the ceremony in which a guest who is not a Lutheran should *not* participate?
Who is welcome to receive Holy Communion varies among Lutheran churches. The worship bulletin will usually state the policy for visitors.

If not disruptive to the ceremony, it is okay to:
◪ **Take pictures?** Only with prior permission from the pastor.
◪ **Use a flash?** Only with prior permission from the pastor.
◪ **Use a video camera?** Only with prior permission from the pastor.
◪ **Use a tape recorder?** Only with prior permission from the pastor.

Will contributions to the church be collected at the ceremony?
No.

THE INTERMENT

Should guests attend the interment?
Yes.

Whom should one ask for directions?
Either join the funeral procession or ask the funeral director for directions.

What happens at the graveside?
The casket is carried to the grave. Prayers and readings are offered. The pastor blesses the earth placed on the casket and blesses those gathered at the graveside.

Do guests who are not Lutherans participate at the graveside service?
If this does not conflict with their own religious beliefs, they recite the Lord's Prayer and join in these responses to other prayers: "The Lord be with you" and "And also with you."

COMFORTING THE BEREAVED

Is it appropriate to visit the home of the bereaved after the funeral?
Yes, more than once is appropriate. Share in the conversation and refreshments.

Will there be a religious service at the home of the bereaved?
No.

Will food be served?
Possibly. If food is served, wait for the saying of grace before eating. It would be impolite not to eat, unless you have dietary restrictions. (If so, mention these to your host or hostess.) There may be alcoholic beverages, depending on the family's custom.

How soon after the funeral will a mourner usually return to a normal work schedule?
The bereaved often stay home from work for several days.

How soon after the funeral will a mourner usually return to a normal social schedule?
Not for several weeks after the funeral.

Are there mourning customs to which a friend who is not a Lutheran should be sensitive?
No.

Are there rituals for observing the anniversary of the death?

While there are no specific such rituals, some congregations remember the first year anniversary in prayers in church.

23

Mennonite/Amish

HISTORY AND BELIEFS

There are nearly 20 organized groups of Mennonites in North America. They vary in life style and religious practice, but all originate from the same sixteenth century Anabaptist movement in Europe. The Anabaptist movement began when a small group of religious reformers claimed Protestant reformers were not sufficiently "radical." They also differed with mainstream Protestants on the timing of baptism. Protestants called for baptism of infants, while Anabaptists mandated that one should be baptized after reaching an "age of accountability," which usually begins with early adolescence and confers the ability to profess belief for one's self.

The name "Mennonite" is derived from that of the sixteenth century Dutch Anabaptist leader, Menno Simons. Originally a Roman Catholic priest, Simons became convinced of the falsity of traditional Catholic doctrine and practice of his time, but hesitated at breaking with the Church. He joined the Anabaptists, who were then being persecuted. Grateful for his leadership, the group later adopted a variation on his name.

Over the years, Mennonites have maintained cultural traditions and religious beliefs in differing ways. While this has led to the formation of various Mennonite groups, they hold certain beliefs in common. Among these are that one should emulate Jesus in everyday living and behavior; that the Bible is the inspired word of God; and that Jesus taught the way of peace. Mennonite faith cannot easily be labeled a liberal or a conservative Christian denomination. Rather, it is an alternative to mainstream religion, one that emphasizes evangelism, peace and justice, and that focuses on a holistic approach to Christ's way of personal salvation, while maintaining concern for the physical as well as the spiritual needs of others.

The one over-arching Mennonite belief that differs from all Christian denominations (except for the Society of Friends, or "Quakers," and the Church of the Brethren) is the Church's stand on war and violence. In principle, Mennonites have always been conscientious objectors to war, although individual members have opted for non-combatant roles and even military service. More recently, the broadest emphasis has been placed on "non-violence" so it includes such issues as abortion and capital punishment.

Mennonites began emigrating to North America from Switzerland in the mid-seventeenth century, spreading westward from Pennsylvania and concentrating on rural colonies where they practiced their faith and Swiss culture.

In a second spurt of Mennonite emigration in the late nineteenth century, Mennonites of Dutch, German and Swiss ancestry who had settled in the Ukraine fled Czarist efforts to conscript them into the Russian army. They settled primarily in the Midwestern areas of the United States and Canada. A third and fourth wave of emigration followed both world wars.

An emphasis on missionary work in this century has helped the Church develop so much into an international institution that now more than one-third of adult Mennonites are non-whites. Mennonites combine a keen sense of evangelism with a theology of relief and material aid to people in want. For 75 years, the Mennonite Central Committee, a relief agency operating around the world, has helped the needy and addressed issues of peace and justice.

The Amish, or the Amish-Mennonite, as they are more properly known, originated from a disagreement among European Mennonites regarding "shunning," a practice that had been adopted by the Dutch Mennonites in 1632. Shunning demanded avoiding a fellow Mennonite who had transgressed. In the late 17th century, a Swiss Mennonite, Jacob Ammann, became concerned over laxity in the Swiss and Alsatian Mennonite communities when a woman who had admitted speaking a falsehood was not shunned. Ammann also rejected a prevalent belief that the souls would be saved of those who were sincerely sympathetic to the Mennonite, but did not join the faith. And he urged simplicity and uniformity as a guard against pride. This included the admonition that men not trim their beards. Today, the Amish call for simplicity extends to not using motorized vehicles, partly because of concerns that they could take Amish too far from their own community.

The group that eventually coalesced around Ammann and his teachings called themselves "Amish" in his honor. The first Amish arrived in North America around 1727, but a congregation was not formed until 1749 in

Berks County, Pennsylvania. By the mid-19th century, there were significant Amish communities in Lancaster and Chester counties in Pennsylvania and in Holmes County, Ohio, as well as in Waterloo County, Ontario, Canada.

The largest Mennonite and Amish denominations in the United States are the Mennonite Church, with 1,004 churches and almost 91,000 members; the Old Order Amish Church, which is widely known for its resistance to modern technology, has 898 churches and almost 81,000 members; and the General Conference Mennonite Church, with 270 churches and 36,685 members.

Smaller, more traditional denominations include the Beachy Amish Mennonite (138 churches; 8,399 members); the Fellowship of Evangelical Bible Churches (37 churches; 4,039 members); and the Reformed Mennonite Church (10 churches; 346 members).

The largest Mennonite and Amish denominations in Canada include the Conference of Mennonites in Canada–General Conference, Mennonite Church, with 223 churches and 33,123 members (including 8,145 members from the Mennonite Church); the General Conference of the Mennonite Brethren Churches–Canada, with 207 churches and 28,368 members; and various Russian Mennonite immigrant groups numbering 20,164 members.

Smaller, more traditional denominations include Old Order Mennonite (5,763 members); Beachy Amish and Old Order Amish (1,612 members); Mennonite Church (independent and unaffiliated groups, 2,187 members).

U.S. churches: 2,455
U.S. membership: 266,693
(data from the 1998 Yearbook of American and Canadian Churches*)*

Canadian churches: 3,126
Canadian membership: 91,217
(data compiled from Mennonite World Conference Directory, 1994; Mennonite Year Book, 1997; *and* 1998 Yearbook of American and Canadian Churches)

FUNERALS AND MOURNING

Mennonites and Amish regard death as part of God's plan. Those who die as believers will share in the resurrection and be with Christ forever. The righteous will inherit the Kingdom of God; the unrighteous shall suffer the anguish of eternal hell. At the resurrection, Christ will create a new heaven and a new earth in which righteousness will reign.

A funeral or memorial service in a Mennonite or Amish church celebrates the life of the deceased and their passing into eternal spiritual life after death.

The funeral service may last between 30 and 90 minutes.

BEFORE THE CEREMONY

How soon after the death does the funeral usually take place?

Two to three days.

What should a non-Mennonite or non-Amish do upon hearing of the death of a member of that faith?

In most denominations, one may telephone or visit the bereaved or send them a card or letter to express condolences and concern for the family. Depending on one's relationship with the bereaved, one may also personally visit them.

APPROPRIATE ATTIRE

Men: In more conservative denominations, such as the Beachy Amish Mennonite, a suit jacket is worn, but without a tie. In other denominations, such as the General Conference Mennonite Church or the General Conference of Mennonite Brethren, a suit or a jacket and tie are worn.

No Mennonite denomination requires a head covering.

Women: In more conservative denominations, such as the Beachy Amish Mennonite, women are expected to wear dresses that cover their arms and have hems that reach below their knees. Neither open-toed shoes nor modest jewelry are permissible. Church members cover their heads, but visitors are not expected to do so. No head covering is required.

In less conservative denominations, such as the General Conference Mennonite Church and the General Conference of Mennonite Brethren, women may wear a dress or a skirt and blouse. Clothing need not cover women's arms nor hems reach below the knees. Open-toed shoes and modest jewelry are permissible. No head covering is required.

Dark, somber, solid colors are advised for all denominations.

GIFTS

Is it appropriate to send flowers or make a contribution?

Do not send flowers to bereaved who belong to more conservative denominations, such as the Beachy Amish Mennonite Church. For funerals in other Mennonite denominations, flowers are appropriate. These may be sent to the home of the bereaved upon hearing of the death or to the church where the funeral will be held. Contributions may be made in memory of the deceased to a cause designated by the bereaved family.

Is it appropriate to send food?

Food may be sent to the home of the bereaved upon hearing of the death or after the funeral. It is recommended to send prepared foods that can be refrigerated until needed.

THE CEREMONY

Where will the ceremony take place?

Usually in the main sanctuary of the church; sometimes in a funeral home.

When should guests arrive and where should they sit?

Arrive shortly before the time for which the funeral has been called. Ushers will advise guests where to sit.

If arriving late, are there times when a guest should *not* enter the ceremony?

Do not enter while prayers are being recited.

Will the bereaved family be present at the church or funeral home before the ceremony?

No.

Is there a traditional greeting for the family?

Express your concern by using such phrases as "My condolences to you" or "I want to express my sympathy to you."

Will there be an open casket?

Often in some Mennonite or Amish denominations. Rarely in the General Conference of Mennonite Brethren.

Is a guest expected to view the body?

Usually.

What is appropriate behavior upon viewing the body?

Pause in front of the casket or walk slowly past it, then sit in the sanctuary where the funeral will be held.

Who are the major officiants at the ceremony and what do they do?

- *The pastor,* who presides.
- *The song leader and/or musicians,* who lead or provide music.

What books are used?

Various translations of the Bible are used. In the Mennonite Brethren Church, the most common versions are the New International Version and the New Revised Standard Version. More conservative denominations may use the King James Version.

In each denomination, various hymnals are used. The Mennonite Church and the General Conference Mennonite Church use *Hymnal: A Worship Book* (Newton, Kans.: Faith and Life Press, 1992). The Mennonite Brethren Church uses *Worship Together* (Fresno, Calif.: The Board of Faith and Life, The General Conference of Mennonite Brethren Churches, 1995).

To indicate the order of the ceremony:

A program may be provided. If not, periodic announcements will be made by the pastor.

Will a guest who is neither Mennonite nor Amish be expected to do anything other than sit?

Guests who do not belong to these Churches are expected to stand with congregants when they arise. If it does not violate their religious beliefs, it is optional for them to sing and read prayers aloud with the congregants.

Are there any parts of the ceremony in which a guest who is neither Mennonite nor Amish should *not* participate?

No.

If not disruptive to the ceremony, is it okay to:

- **Take pictures?** No.
- **Use a flash?** No.
- **Use a video camera?** No.
- **Use a tape recorder?** No.

Will contributions to the church be collected at the ceremony?

No.

THE INTERMENT

Should guests attend the interment?

This is entirely optional. Often, the interment is intended only for family and close friends, and sometimes only for family.

Whom should one ask for directions?

An usher.

What happens at the graveside?

The pastor recites some opening words and a brief sermon, Scripture is read, and the casket is lowered into the ground and covered.

Do guests who are neither Mennonite nor Amish participate at the graveside ceremony?

No, they are simply present.

COMFORTING THE BEREAVED

Is it appropriate to visit the home of the bereaved after the funeral?

Yes, for anywhere from five to 20 minutes. It is appropriate to inquire about how the family is doing during this time of grief. Unless one is a close friend or a family member, it is advised to avoid asking for details about the illness and the death of the deceased.

Will there be a religious service at the home of the bereaved?

No.

Will food be served?

Possibly, but no alcoholic beverages.

How soon after the funeral will a mourner usually return to a normal work schedule?

The Church has no set ritual, but it is common for the bereaved to be absent from work for a few days to a whole week after the funeral.

How soon after the funeral will a mourner usually return to a normal social schedule?

The Church has no set ritual, but it is common for the bereaved to abstain from socializing from a few days to a whole week after the funeral.

Are there mourning customs to which a friend who is neither Mennonite nor Amish should be sensitive?

No.

Are there rituals for observing the anniversary of the death?

Cards remembering the deceased are appreciated upon the one-year anniversary of the death.

24

Methodist

HISTORY AND BELIEFS

The Methodist movement began in 18th-century England under the preaching of John Wesley, an Anglican priest who was a prodigious evangelical preacher, writer and organizer. While a student at Oxford University, he and his brother, Charles, led the Holy Club of devout students, whom scoffers called the "Methodists."

Wesley's teachings affirmed the freedom of human will as promoted by grace. He saw each person's depth of sin matched by the height of sanctification to which the Holy Spirit, the empowering spirit of God, can lead persons of faith.

Although Wesley remained an Anglican and disavowed attempts to form a new church, Methodism eventually became another church body. During a conference in Baltimore, Maryland, in 1784, the Methodist Church was founded as an ecclesiastical organization and the first Methodist bishop in the United States was elected.

The Methodist movement was first represented in Canada by Laurence Coughlan, who began to preach in Newfoundland in 1766. It wasn't until 1884, however, that the Methodist Church was formed in Canada from the merger of the Methodist Episcopal Church and smaller Methodist bodies, with the Wesleyan Methodist Church, the Conference of Eastern British America and the New Connexion Church, which had united in 1874. The Free Methodists, entering from the U.S. in 1876, were few in number and have remained separate.

In the nineteenth century, strong missionary programs helped plant Methodism abroad. Methodist missionaries from America followed their

British colleagues to India and Africa, where they founded new churches. Americans and Canadians also founded churches in East Asia, Latin America and continental Europe.

Local Methodist churches are called "charges." Their ministers are appointed by the bishop at an annual conference, and each church elects its own administrative board, which initiates planning and sets local goals and policies.

There are about 125 Methodist denominations around the globe and 23 separate Methodist bodies in the United States. Of these, the United Methodist Church is numerically the largest.

In Canada, the Methodist Church ceased to exist as a separate denomination in 1925, when it joined with Congregationalists and the majority of Presbyterian churches to form the United Church of Canada. The Free Methodist Church in Canada, which was incorporated in 1927 and which gained full autonomy from the U.S. parent denomination in 1990, remains intact.

U.S. churches: 36,361
U.S. membership: 8.5 million
(data from the 1998 Yearbook of American and Canadian Churches*)*

Canadian churches: 129
Canadian membership: 5,360
(data from the 1998 Yearbook of American and Canadian Churches*)*

FUNERALS AND MOURNING

The United Methodist Church affirms that life is eternal and that, in faith, one can look forward to life with God after death.

United Methodists have diverse beliefs about afterlife and are generally content to look forward to it as a glorious mystery. Funerals have as their purposes: 1) expressing grief and comforting one another in our bereavement; 2) celebrating the life of the deceased; and 3) affirming faith in life with God after death. Which of these is most emphasized at the funeral depends on the circumstances of the death and the extent of the faith of the deceased.

BEFORE THE CEREMONY

How soon after the death will the funeral usually take place?
Usually within two to three days.

What should a non-Methodist do upon hearing of the death of a member of that faith?

Telephone or visit the bereaved.

APPROPRIATE ATTIRE

Men: Jacket and tie. No head covering is required.

Women: A dress. Open-toed shoes and modest jewelry are permissible. No head covering is required.

There are no rules regarding colors of clothing, but somber, dark colors are recommended for men and women.

GIFTS

Is it appropriate to send flowers or make a contribution?

Yes. Send flowers to the home of the bereaved. Contributions are also optional. The recommended charity may be mentioned in the deceased's obituary.

Is it appropriate to send food?

Yes. Send it to the home of the bereaved.

THE CEREMONY

Where will the ceremony take place?

At a church or funeral home.

When should guests arrive and where should they sit?

Arrive early. Ushers will advise where to sit.

If arriving late, are there times when a guest should *not* enter the ceremony?

No.

Will the bereaved family be present at the church or funeral home before the ceremony?

Possibly.

Is there a traditional greeting for the family?

Simply express your condolences.

Will there be an open casket?

Usually.

Is a guest expected to view the body?
This is entirely optional.

What is appropriate behavior upon viewing the body?
Silent prayer.

Who are the major officiants at the ceremony and what do they do?
■ *A pastor*, who officiates.

To indicate the order of the ceremony:
A program will be provided.

Will a guest who is not a Methodist be expected to do anything other than sit?
No.

Are there any parts of the service in which a guest who is not a Methodist should *not* participate?
No.

If not disruptive to the ceremony, is it okay to:
■ **Take pictures?** No.
■ **Use a flash?** No.
■ **Use a video camera?** No.
■ **Use a tape recorder?** No.

Will contributions to the church be collected at the ceremony?
No.

THE INTERMENT

Should guests attend the interment?
Yes.

Whom should one ask for directions?
The funeral director.

What happens at the graveside?
Prayers are recited by the pastor and the body is committed to the ground. If there has been a cremation, which is done privately before the service, the ashes are either buried or put in a vault. Military or fraternal rites may be part of the graveside service.

Do guests who are not Methodists participate at the graveside ceremony?
No. They are simply present.

COMFORTING THE BEREAVED

Is it appropriate to visit the home of the bereaved after the funeral?

Yes, at any mutually convenient time. How long one stays depends on one's closeness to the bereaved. Typically, one stays about 30 to 45 minutes.

Will there be a religious service at the home of the bereaved?

No.

Will food be served?

No.

How soon after the funeral will a mourner usually return to a normal work schedule?

This is entirely at the discretion of the bereaved.

How soon after the funeral will a mourner usually return to a normal social schedule?

This is entirely at the discretion of the bereaved.

Are there mourning customs to which a friend who is not a Methodist should be sensitive?

No.

Are there rituals for observing the anniversary of the death?

There may be a service commemorating the deceased.

25

Mormon (Church of Jesus Christ of Latter-day Saints)

HISTORY AND BELIEFS

The Church of Jesus Christ of Latter-day Saints, the largest indigenous American religious group, was founded by Joseph Smith in the early 19th century. Living in upstate New York, Smith had a vision in 1820 in which God and Jesus Christ appeared to him. Three years later, the angel Moroni told him of the location of gold tablets containing God's revelations. In 1830, Smith published a translation of these revelations entitled *The Book of Mormon*. He soon became the "seer, translator, prophet and apostle" of a group committed to restoring the church established centuries before by Christ.

Latter-day Saints stressed the coming of Christ's Kingdom to earth and encouraged others to adhere to the teachings of the Savior.

Smith's group moved first to Ohio, and then to Missouri, where violence ensued prompted by their polygamy and their anti-slavery stance. Persecution forced the group to move to Illinois, where they built their own city and named it Nauvoo. In 1844, while imprisoned for destroying an opposition printing press, Smith was killed by a mob that attacked the jail.

Schisms erupted amid the subsequent leadership vacuum and concern over polygamy, a practice that Smith had said in 1843 had come to him in a vision and which became Church doctrine in 1852. Most Latter-day Saints followed the leadership of Brigham Young, who led them into the Great Salt Lake area of what is now Utah. Latter-day Saints are headquartered there to this day.

While many Latter-day Saints' beliefs are similar to orthodox Christian ideas, Smith uniquely taught that God, although omniscient, has a material body. He taught that through repentance and baptism by immersion, anyone can gain entrance to Christ's earthly kingdom. Through "proxies" who receive baptism in a Latter-day Saints' temple, the dead may also share in the highest of post-mortal rewards or blessings.

The Church teaches that men and women are equal in the eyes of the Lord and that they cannot achieve the highest eternal rewards without each other.

The charge given by Jesus to Matthew, "Go ye unto all the world" to share the teachings of His gospel, motivates the Church's 57,000 full-time missionaries around the world. Most are college-age males who serve for two years at their own expense. Their success has led to the church currently having more than 25,000 congregations in 160 nations and territories around the world.

In addition to churches, where worship services are conducted, temples are located around the world. These are closed on Sundays, but open every other day of the week for marriages and other sacred ordinances. Only faithful members of the Church may enter a temple.

U.S. churches and temples: 10,000+
U.S. membership: 4.3 million

(1995 data from The Church of Jesus Christ of Latter-day Saints)

Canadian churches and temples: 450+
Canadian membership: 150,000

(1997 data from The Church of Jesus Christ of Latter-day Saints)

FUNERALS AND MOURNING

Latter-day Saints believe that all who have ever lived on earth are literally the spiritual children of God and resided with him in a pre-mortal existence. The same with those who ever will live on earth. Through the resurrection of Jesus, all will be resurrected and through atonement and obedience to His gospel, all have the opportunity for salvation.

A Latter-day Saint funeral is a service in itself. The length of the service varies according to the program outlined by the family, but it usually lasts about 60 to 90 minutes.

BEFORE THE CEREMONY

How soon after the death does the funeral usually take place?

There is no set limit, although typically it occurs within one week after the death. The timing of the funeral is solely the choice of the immediate family and depends on circumstances.

What should someone who is not a Latter-day Saint do upon hearing of the death of a member of that faith?

Visit, telephone or write to the family, expressing your condolences and offering your assistance, if needed.

APPROPRIATE ATTIRE:

Men: A suit or sport jacket and tie. No head covering required.

Women: A dress, suit or a skirt and blouse. No head covering required, but the overall fashion statement should be conservative and dignified. Hems should be near the knees. Open-toed shoes and modest jewelry are permissible.

Modest and dignified clothing is appreciated.

GIFTS

Is it appropriate to send flowers or make a contribution?

It is appropriate, but not expected to do either. These may be sent, before or after the funeral, to the funeral itself (which may be held in a church or a funeral home) or to the home of the bereaved.

Is it appropriate to send food?

Food for the bereaved family members is usually prepared and organized by the woman's organization of the local congregation.

THE CEREMONY

Where will the ceremony take place?

Either in a church or a funeral home or at the graveside.

When should guests arrive and where should they sit?

Arrive at the time for which the service has been called. Sit wherever you wish.

If arriving late, are there times when a guest should *not* enter the ceremony?
No.

Will the bereaved family be present at the church or the funeral home before the ceremony?
Usually.

Is there a traditional greeting for the family?
No. Just offer your condolences.

Will there be an open casket?
Sometimes. This is done at the choice of the family.

Is a guest expected to view the body?
Viewing is entirely optional.

What is appropriate behavior upon viewing the body?
Observe it with dignity and reverence.

Who are the major officiants at the ceremony and what do they do?
- *The officer of the church* who conducts the service. This person is chosen by the family, but is typically the bishop of the congregation to which the deceased belonged.
- *Speakers* who deliver eulogies.

What books are used?
Speakers will use Scriptures. Hymn books may be used by the congregation.

To indicate the order of the ceremony:
A program may be distributed.

Will a guest who is not a Latter-day Saint be expected to do anything other than sit?
No.

Are there any parts of the ceremony in which a guest who is not a Latter-day Saint should *not* participate?
No.

If not disruptive to the ceremony, is it okay to:
- **Take pictures?** No.
- **Use a flash?** No.
- **Use a video camera?** No.
- **Use a tape recorder?** Possibly, if it can be done with discretion.

Will contributions to the church be collected at the ceremony?
No.

THE INTERMENT

Should guests attend the interment?
Yes, unless it is a private interment, which is rare. If the burial is private, attendance is only by invitation.

Whom should one ask for directions?
The director of the funeral home or the person who officiated at the service may give directions from the pulpit. Also, the printed program may have directions.

What happens at the graveside?
The grave is dedicated in a prayer offered by a lay priest, who is usually (but not necessarily) a member of the family of the deceased. Then the deceased is buried.

Do guests who are not Latter-day Saints participate at the graveside ceremony?
No, they are simply present.

COMFORTING THE BEREAVED

Is it appropriate to visit the home of the bereaved after the funeral?
Yes, if one wishes to do so.

Will there be a religious service at the home of the bereaved?
No.

Will food be served?
There may be light food, but no alcoholic beverages. At the choice of the hosts, a grace or benediction may be said before eating.

How soon after the funeral will a mourner usually return to a normal work schedule?
There is no set time. Absence from work is at the discretion of the mourner.

How soon after the funeral will a mourner usually return to a normal social schedule?
There is no set time. Absence from social events is at the discretion of the mourner.

Are there mourning customs to which a friend who is not a Latter-day Saint should be sensitive?

No.

Are there rituals for observing the anniversary of the death?

No.

26

Native American/First Nations

Native American/First Nations religion does not exist as a single, readily identifiable faith. (In practice, few Native Peoples use the word "religion" to describe their traditional ceremonies and practices. The term is used here to help those outside the community relate in some way to the understandings and "the way of life" of aboriginal/indigenous peoples.) Indigenous Americans (whom United States law recognizes as American Indians and Alaska Natives) and First Nations peoples in Canada have diverse and rich religious traditions. Although it is impossible to generalize about the diverse ceremonial practices of Native Americans/First Nations peoples, some suggestions regarding respectful behavior at their religious ceremonies can be made based on the beliefs and values that are the foundation of their deeply spiritual worldviews.

Because these beliefs and values are intimately related to Native people's sense of the sacred, they directly influence what would count as respectful and appropriate behavior for those invited to attend most Native American/First Nations religious ceremonies. Since even those who are well-intentioned are often not aware of these beliefs and values, they may behave in ways that Native Peoples interpret as disrespectful toward their religious ceremonies and practices. Diverse religious traditions explain why those who have briefly visited—or actually lived—with Native Peoples report that they have encountered a people who are deeply connected to the sacred.

According to the 1990 United States census, American Indian and Alaska Native population totals approximately 1.9 million. Although this is roughly one percent of the total population of the United States, the more than 500 nations of the Native Peoples represent approximately 90 percent of the ethnic diversity in the United States. Among Native Peoples, there are nine major language families with almost 200 distinct dialects. From a constitutional viewpoint, the First Americans are citizens of their own various nations as well as of the United States.

Many First Nations people in Canada do not consider themselves to be "American" nor, for that matter, citizens of Canada. They see themselves as people of First Nations communities such as "Whata First Nations," or "Shawanaga First Nations," or "Peepeekisis First Nations." "Indian" is a term specifically used by the government of Canada to define certain aboriginal people mentioned in the Indian Act of 1867 and excludes many people of aboriginal ancestry. There are 53 aboriginal languages in Canada, including Inuit and Metis languages.

If you consider the geographic and cultural diversity of the five largest tribal groups in the United States alone—the Cherokee in North Carolina and Oklahoma, the Navajo in Arizona and New Mexico, the Chippewa of the Northern and Great Lakes regions, the Sioux (which include the Lakota, Dakota and Nakota) spread across the Northern Plains, and the Choctaw in Mississippi and Oklahoma—you begin to grasp why it is impossible to generalize about the cultural practices and specifically, the religious ceremonies and practices of Native Americans/First Nations peoples.

HISTORY AND BELIEFS

Over the last 500 years, Native Peoples have endured what they consider to be almost constant disrespect. Recognizing this unpleasant legacy will help those desiring to visit Native American religious ceremonies understand why many Native Peoples are wary about sharing the most important elements of their identity with those who do not share their faith.

In 1879, for instance, the Carlisle Indian Boarding School was created in Carlisle, Pennsylvania. This was the first of what would eventually be dozens of off-reservation boarding schools designed to "solve" the "Indian Problem." In the late 1870s, the federal government assumed that the "Indian Problem" could be eradicated by education built around creating institutions dedicated to the complete cultural assimilation of First American boys and girls and erasing their beliefs, values and culture. Similar policies were enacted by the federal government of Canada.

Not surprisingly, given the centrality of the sacred to Native culture and identity, completely eradicating their indigenous religious and spiritual traditions was deemed a prerequisite for successful "education." Christian clergy often ran these schools since "civilizing" these children meant converting them to Christianity.

Understanding just this small part of the history of Native Peoples when attending their religious events and ceremonies can help you appreciate the intrinsically communitarian and private nature of their religious practices.

Native American/First Nations religion is primarily about experience, not about theology or doctrine.

It is simultaneously a personal and a profoundly communal experience. The nearly universal rule among Native Peoples that explains this is that ceremonies, customs and various cultural traditions, which are all ways of exercising spirituality, are, at their core, *community* activities for community members. Religious experience is profoundly shaped by one's membership and involvement in a community and one's life at a specific geographic place in relation to the whole of Creation.

Native spirituality denies the dichotomies common to Western religions.

The Western dualisms of supernatural vs. natural, spiritual vs. earthly/worldly, sacred vs. profane and heaven vs. hell do not easily fit with Native spirituality. Unlike religious traditions that see life on earth filled primarily with evil, toil and suffering, Native spirituality perceives the world as deeply endowed with the sacred power of the Creator.

Native languages, oral traditions, symbols, ceremonial objects and ceremonial practices speak directly to the recognition that humans are surrounded by the spiritual power of the Creator. Traditional prayers and ceremonies embody the widely held belief that we are imbued with one small part of the spirit of our Creator.

For Native peoples, the entire natural world is full of the sacred.

Each living part of Creation, and especially the places important to each tribe or village, serve as but one entrance into the power of the sacred. With this recognition of the complexity of Creation and the Creator's power comes the obvious realization that humans are but one part of the natural world, and not necessarily a privileged part or even the only "persons" inhabiting the earth.

Consequently, the high degree of religious diversity among Native Peoples reflects another widely shared element in traditional Native religious practices.

Native religious activities are almost universally attached to specific places.

These sacred sites mark the appropriate place for the enactment of certain ceremonies and religious activities. Even Native Peoples who experienced painful removal and relocation from their indigenous homelands in the eighteenth and nineteenth centuries found sacred sites in places new to them where their religious traditions could be carried out.

Most Native sacred sites are not analogous to a church, a temple or a shrine, which are consecrated as sacred by humans and built from blueprints, plans and drawings. Instead, Native ceremonial sites are often located on the land where specific tribes identify their spiritual center.

The places Native Peoples identify as their respective homelands and the communities that exist there are at the center of their religious experience. At the most fundamental level, the rich spirituality of Native peoples is literally "grounded" in their experience of the natural world as the cathedral of their Creator.

Native religious traditions are profoundly holistic.

Native faiths or teachings often refer to Creation itself as a complex web of life or a sacred circle in which all aspects of the natural world connect to each other. Because of this, humanity, in most Native worldviews, does not hold a privileged place above the rest of Creation, but is understood to be only a small part of Creation.

In many Native worldviews, many "persons" other than humans inhabit the world. Native Peoples attribute the qualities of power, consciousness and volition generally identified with the Western view of personhood to many living things. Consequently, Native Peoples perceive the environment to be inhabited with four-legged "persons" that swim in the water or winged "persons" that fly. To the Native way of thinking, these "persons" are also part of the moral and political community. Most importantly, they are also part of the spiritual community. In Native thought, to recognize that the earth is sacred is also to acknowledge all the "members" of our many respective communities.

The holistic nature of Native worldviews and spirituality gives a centrality to the idea of balance in one's life and in the world. Living in a good, healthy, beautiful way requires one to recognize that growth and success are achieved by integrating psychological, physical and spiritual well-being.

Native religious traditions openly acknowledge the existence of unseen powers.

Forces and mysteries exist that First Peoples experience and recognize, but cannot see or fully understand or comprehend. These sacred powers are not mysteries that need to be solved, but exist because humanity cannot know and understand everything about Creation or the Creator.

Native religions have no tradition of proselytizing.

Spiritual leaders and wisdom keepers do not undertake missionary activities. Their dependence on experience and on understanding the diversity of the circle of life makes it perfectly acceptable—and, perhaps to them, inevitable—that people from different places will have different religions. Consequently, First Peoples were always confused by other people who insisted they be just like them. This appreciation for the biological and cultural diversity of Mother Earth and her children explains Native respect for people's different ways of honoring the Creator and Creation. It also explains why Native people are often wary of those so interested in their traditions when the Creator gave all human beings a knowledge of the sacred.

FUNERALS AND MOURNING

Many Native peoples believe that death is the beginning of another journey, into the next world. Since one's spirit often needs help to make this journey, strict rules often govern the behavior of the living relatives of the deceased to ensure their loved one a good start in his or her journey to the other world. Some Potawatomi continue their ancient tradition of setting a place for the spirit of the deceased person at a funeral feast, in order for the spirit of the deceased to partake of the "spirit" food.

Among the Yuchi, who are politically recognized as part of the Creek Nation of Oklahoma and number less than 1,000, Christian burial customs are occasionally interwoven with Yuchi traditions. These may include placing such items as a hunting rifle, a blanket, some tobacco and other personal items in an adult male's coffin before interment. This reflects the Yuchi belief that one's journey in an afterlife is not significantly different from our present life.

At a Native funeral, express your sympathy and empathy to the bereaved. While Native beliefs assert that death is not necessarily the termination of life, the bereaved still mourn the absence from this life of the one who has died.

Many tribes restrict what bereaved relatives can eat and/or what kind of activities they can engage in after the death of a loved one. This represents a sacrifice by the living for those who have moved on in the circle of life.

27

Orthodox Churches

(Includes the Antiochian Orthodox Church; the Carpatho-Russian Orthodox Church; the Greek Orthodox Church; the Orthodox Church in North America [also known as the Russian Orthodox Church]; the Romanian Orthodox Church; the Serbian Orthodox Church; and the Ukrainian Orthodox Church. An entire chapter is devoted to Greek Orthodoxy in this book since it is the Orthodox denomination with the largest membership in the United States.)

HISTORY AND BELIEFS

The Orthodox Church, or the eastern half of the Christian Church, was formed in 1054 A.D. In that year the Great Schism occurred, causing a complete breakdown in communication and relations between the Roman Catholic Church, based in Rome, and the Orthodox Church, based in Constantinople. When the patriarchs of the various Orthodox churches meet, they are presided over by the Patriarch of Constantinople (present-day Istanbul), who is considered to be the "first among equals."

The term "Orthodox" is used to reflect adherents' belief that they believe and worship God correctly. Essentially, Orthodox Christians consider their beliefs similar to those of other Christian traditions, but believe that the balance and integrity of the teachings of Jesus' 12 apostles have been preserved inviolate by their Church.

Orthodoxy holds that the eternal truths of God's saving revelation in Jesus Christ are preserved in the living tradition of the Church under the guidance and inspiration of the Holy Spirit, which is the empowering spirit of God and the particular endowment of the Church. While the Holy

Scriptures are the written testimony of God's revelation, Holy Tradition is the all-encompassing experience of the Church under the guidance and direction of the Holy Spirit.

Orthodox churches are hierarchical and self-governing. They are also called "Eastern," because they stem from countries that shared the Christian heritage of the eastern part of the Roman and Byzantine Empire. They completely agree on matters of faith, despite a diversity of culture, language and the lands in which they flowered before arriving in North America.

Orthodox churches in North America today include:

- The American Carpatho-Russian Orthodox Greek Catholic Church, a self-governing diocese formalized in 1938 whose founders came from present-day Slovakia.

- The Antiochian Orthodox Christian Archdiocese of North America, an Arabic-language church whose first parish in North America was founded in Brooklyn in 1895. The Church in Antioch traces its origins to the days of the apostles, Peter and Paul, and to the Syrian city of Antioch in which the Book of Acts says the followers of Jesus Christ were first called "Christians."

- The Greek Orthodox Archdiocese of America, which is under the jurisdiction of the Ecumenical Patriarchate of Constantinople in Istanbul.

- The Orthodox Church in America, which was given full, independent status by the Russian Orthodox Church in 1970. It is comprised of ethnic Russians, Bulgarians, Albanians and Romanians.

- The Romanian Orthodox Church in America, which was founded in 1929 and was granted ecclesiastical autonomy in 1950 from the church in Romania.

- The Serbian Orthodox Church in the U.S.A. and Canada, which was created in 1921 and whose patriarchal seat is in Belgrade, Yugoslavia.

- The Ukrainian Orthodox Church of America, which was organized in 1928; and the Ukrainian Orthodox Church of Canada, which was organized in 1918, and which is the largest Ukrainian Orthodox Church beyond the borders of the Ukraine.

U.S. churches:

Antiochian Orthodox: 16
Carpatho-Russian Orthodox: 78
Greek Orthodox: 532
Romanian Orthodox: 37
Russian Orthodox (also known as the Orthodox Church
in America, or the OCA): 600

Serbian Orthodox: 68
Ukrainian Orthodox: 27

U.S. membership:

Antiochian Orthodox: 50,000
Carpatho-Russian Orthodox: 12,541
Greek Orthodox: 2 million
Romanian Orthodox: 65,000
Russian Orthodox (also known as the Orthodox Church
in America, or the OCA): 2 million
Serbian Orthodox: 67,000
Ukrainian Orthodox: 5,000

*(data from the respective denominations and from
the* 1998 Yearbook of American and Canadian Churches*)*

Canadian churches:

Antiochian Orthodox: 15
Greek Orthodox: 76
Romanian Orthodox: Not available
Russian Orthodox (also known as the Orthodox Church in
America): 606
Serbian Orthodox: Not available
Ukrainian Orthodox: 258

Canadian membership:

Antiochian Orthodox: 100,000
Greek Orthodox: 350,000
Romanian Orthodox: Not available
Russian Orthodox (also known as the Orthodox Church
in America): 1,000,000
Serbian Orthodox: Not available
Ukrainian Orthodox: 120,000

(data from the 1998 Yearbook of American and Canadian Churches*)*

FUNERALS AND MOURNING

Orthodox churches believe that death is the separation of the soul (the spiritual dimension of each human being) from the body (the physical dimension of each human being). Upon death, we immediately begin to experience a foretaste of heaven and hell. This experience, known as the partial judgment, is based on the general character of our lives regarding behavior, character and communion with God.

At some unknown time in the future, the churches teach, Jesus Christ will return and inaugurate a new era in which His kingdom shall be established. The final judgment will then occur. In our resurrected existence, we will either live eternally in heaven in communion with God, or eternally in hell and out of communion with God.

The 30- to 60-minute funeral ceremony is not part of a larger service, although in the American Carpatho-Russian Church, the Eucharistic liturgy (essentially the Sunday morning worship service) is often celebrated in addition to the funeral service. This is done at the discretion of the bereaved family and may cause the entire ceremony to last up to 90 minutes.

BEFORE THE CEREMONY

How soon after the death does the funeral usually take place?

Usually within two to three days.

What should a non-Orthodox do upon hearing of the death of a member of that faith?

It is appropriate to visit or telephone the bereaved at their home before the funeral to express condolences and recall the life of the deceased. When visiting a bereaved family before the service, a traditional greeting to a member of the Antiochian Orthodox Church is "May his [or her] memory be eternal."

APPROPRIATE ATTIRE

Men: A jacket and tie. No head covering is required.

Women: A dress or a skirt and blouse. Clothing should cover the arms and hems should reach below the knee. A head covering is not required. Open-toed shoes and modest jewelry may be worn.

Somber, dark colors are recommended for both men and women.

GIFTS

Is it appropriate to send flowers or make a contribution?

It is appropriate to send flowers to the funeral home before the funeral. It is also appropriate to make a contribution in the memory of the deceased to either his or her church or to a fund or charity designated by the family of the deceased.

Is it appropriate to send food?

Yes. This is ordinarily sent to the home of the bereaved upon either initially hearing about the death or after the funeral.

THE CEREMONY

Where will the ceremony take place?

Either at a funeral home or at the house of worship of the deceased.

When should guests arrive and where should they sit?

Arrive early or at the time for which the ceremony has been called. Ushers will advise guests where to sit.

If arriving late, are there times when a guest should *not* enter the ceremony?

No.

Will the bereaved family be present at the church or funeral home before the ceremony?

Yes.

Is there a traditional greeting for the family?

In the Antiochian Orthodox church, a traditional greeting is "May God give you the strength to bear your loss." In other Orthodox churches, express your condolences.

Will there be an open casket?

Yes.

Is a guest expected to view the body?

This is optional.

What is appropriate behavior upon viewing the body?

Stand briefly in front of the casket and offer a silent prayer. A Christian might also cross himself or herself and kiss the cross or icon resting on the casket.

Who are the major officiants at the ceremony and what do they do?

- *A bishop,* who is the chief celebrant.
- *A priest,* who may be the chief celebrant or the assistant to the bishop.
- *The deacon, sub-deacon and altar server,* all of whom assist the bishop or priest.

What books are used?

In most Orthodox churches, only officiating bishops and priests use a text at a funeral ceremony.

To indicate the order of the ceremony:

A program will be distributed.

Will a guest who is not a member of an Orthodox church be expected to do anything other than sit?

Stand when the congregants arise. Kneeling with them is appropriate only if it does not violate a visitor's own religious beliefs. Otherwise, visitors may sit when congregants kneel. Reading prayers aloud and singing with the congregants are optional.

Are there any parts of the ceremony in which a guest who is not a member of an Orthodox church should *not* participate?

No, unless the Eucharistic liturgy is celebrated. In that case, guests who are not Orthodox do not partake in holy communion. This is the high point of the ceremony. It occurs after a priest or bishop advances toward the congregation from the altar, holds up the chalice and says, "With fear of God, with faith and with love, draw ye near." Congregants then go forward to receive communion.

If not disruptive to the ceremony, is it okay to:

◾ **Take pictures?** No.
◾ **Use a flash?** No.
◾ **Use a video camera?** No.
◾ **Use a tape recorder?** No.

Will contributions to the church be collected at the ceremony?

No.

THE INTERMENT

Should guests attend the interment?

This is entirely optional.

Whom should one ask for directions?

Ask the funeral director or a family member.

What happens at the graveside?

There will be a brief prayer ceremony, followed by the officiating priest or bishop usually putting soil on top of the casket so it forms the shape of a cross, and then each person present placing one flower on the casket or spreading soil on the casket. The flowers usually come from those sent to the church for the funeral and then conveyed to the cemetery with the casket. There will be no cremation since this is not permitted in Orthodox churches.

Do guests who are not members of an Orthodox church participate at the graveside ceremony?

No. They are simply present.

COMFORTING THE BEREAVED

Is it appropriate to visit the home of the bereaved after the funeral?

Yes. The tradition in the Orthodox Church in America is to briefly visit the bereaved the same day as the funeral. Religious objects that a visitor may see at such a visit are icons, two-dimensional artistic images of saints; a lighted candle; and burning incense.

Will there be a religious service at the home of the bereaved?

No.

Will food be served?

A Meal of Mercy is often given in the church hall, a restaurant or the home of the deceased shortly after the burial. At the homes of members of the Antiochian Orthodox Church, usually coffee, pastries and/or fruit are served.

How soon after the funeral will a mourner usually return to a normal work schedule?

The bereaved usually stays home from work for one week.

How soon after the funeral will a mourner usually return to a normal social schedule?

The bereaved usually avoids social gatherings for two months. In some cases, especially that of widows, the bereaved may avoid such occasions for a full year after the loss of the deceased.

Are there mourning customs to which a friend who is not a member of an Orthodox church should be sensitive?

Mourners usually avoid social gatherings for the first 40 days after the death. They may also wear only black clothing during this same period.

Are there rituals for observing the anniversary of the death?

A memorial service is held on the Sunday closest to the 40th day after the death. Subsequent memorial services are held on the annual anniversary of the death.

28

Pentecostal Church of God

HISTORY AND BELIEFS

The Pentecostal Church of God was founded in Chicago in 1919 by a group of participants in the then-current Pentecostal revival movement in the United States. Many people involved in the movement spontaneously spoke "in tongues" (or in a language unknown to those speaking it) and claims were made of divine healing that saved lives. Since many of these experiences were associated with the coming of the Holy Spirit (the empowering quality of God) on the Day of Pentecost, participants in the revival were called Pentecostals.

The group that met in Chicago was convinced that a formal Pentecostal church was necessary because many smaller, new, independent Pentecostal houses of worship had become the targets of small-time crooks and con men. They deemed their fledgling Pentecostal Church of God to be indispensable for the Pentecostal revival to continue to thrive.

Pentecostals tenaciously believe in their direct access to God, the Father, and believe prayer can manifest miracles. Worship services are demonstrative and energetic and are often marked by congregants speaking "in tongues." These are languages unknown to the speaker. Such speaking is interpreted as meaning that one is the recipient of the Holy Spirit. Alcohol and tobacco are prohibited to church members.

The Pentecostal Church of God has a combination of representative and congregational forms of government. While local churches are self-governing and elect their own ministers and local leaders, they are also expected to harmoniously function with the Church's district and general organization. The bylaws of local churches cannot conflict with the

Church's district or general bylaws. Each minister is accountable to his or her District Board in matters of faith and conduct.

The Church's biennial General Convention is its highest legislative body. Policy is made and governed by the Church's General Executive Board.

The Church's World Missions Department has ministers in 42 countries and maintains schools in most of these nations, as well. In addition, the Church's Indian Mission Department makes outreach to Native Americans.

Although the Pentecostal Church of God is not present within Canada, the broader Pentecostal tradition is well-represented by the Pentecostal Assemblies of Canada and the Pentecostal Assemblies of Newfoundland, which have a combined total of 1,257 churches, 234,000 members and offices in Mississauga, Ontario, and St. John's, Newfoundland, respectively.

U.S. churches: 1,230
U.S. membership: 111,900
(*data from the* 1998 Yearbook of American and Canadian Churches)

FUNERALS AND MOURNING

Members of the Pentecostal Church of God believe that all Christians who have died will one day rise from their graves and meet the Lord "in the air." Meanwhile, Christians who are still alive will be caught up with those who have risen from their graves and will also be with the Lord. All who have thus joined with God will live forever.

A Pentecostal Church of God funeral usually begins with singing, Scripture reading or prayer. This is followed with hymns, prayer and worship to God, and a sermon and eulogy by the minister.

A ceremony in itself, the funeral ceremony lasts about 30 to 60 minutes.

BEFORE THE CEREMONY

How soon after the death does the funeral usually take place?

Within two to three days.

What should someone who is not a member of the Pentecostal Church of God do upon hearing of the death of a member of that faith?

Telephone or visit the bereaved to offer condolences and sympathies and offer to assist in any way possible.

APPROPRIATE ATTIRE

Men: A jacket and tie. No head covering is required.

Women: A dress or a skirt and blouse. Clothing need not cover the arms and hems need not reach below the knees. Open-toed shoes and modest jewelry are permissible. No head covering is required.

Dark, somber colors for clothing are advised.

GIFTS

Is it appropriate to send flowers or make a contribution?

Flowers may be sent to the funeral home or church where the funeral ceremony is held. Contributions may be sent to a memorial fund determined by the bereaved.

Is it appropriate to send food?

Yes. Send or take it yourself to the home of the bereaved.

THE CEREMONY

Where will the ceremony take place?

Either in a church or a funeral home.

When should guests arrive and where should they sit?

Arrive at the time for which the ceremony has been scheduled. Ushers usually advise guests where to sit.

If arriving late, are there times when a guest should *not* enter the ceremony?

No.

Will the bereaved family be present at the church or funeral home before the ceremony?

Yes.

Is there a traditional greeting for the family?

Just offer your condolences.

Will there be an open casket?

Possibly. This varies with local custom.

Is a guest expected to view the body?

This is optional.

What is appropriate behavior upon viewing the body?

Look into the casket while walking slowly past it, then follow the instructions of the funeral director.

Who are the major officiants at the ceremony and what do they do?

■ *The minister,* who delivers a brief sermon and tribute to the deceased.

■ *Musicians,* who sing two or three songs.

What books are used?

No books are used by mourners or guests.

To indicate the order of the ceremony:

Either a program will be distributed or the minister will make the necessary announcements.

Will a guest who is not a member of the Pentecostal Church of God be expected to do anything other than sit?

Guests of other faiths are expected to stand when other guests arise during the ceremony. While there is usually no kneeling during a funeral ceremony, if there is kneeling, guests of other faiths may remain seated.

Are there any parts of the ceremony in which a guest who is not a member of the Pentecostal Church of God should *not* participate?

No.

If not disruptive to the ceremony, is it okay to:

■ **Take pictures?** No.
■ **Use a flash?** No.
■ **Use a video camera?** No.
■ **Use a tape recorder?** Yes.

Will contributions to the church be collected at the ceremony?

No.

THE INTERMENT

Should guests attend the interment?

Attendance is optional.

Whom should one ask for directions?

An usher or the funeral director or just follow the funeral procession.

What happens at the graveside?

There is usually a prayer and Scripture readings, and sometimes a song. The casket is committed to the ground.

Do guests who are not members of the Pentecostal Church of God participate at the graveside ceremony?

No, they are simply present.

COMFORTING THE BEREAVED

Is it appropriate to visit the home of the bereaved after the funeral?

Yes, if one knows the family well.

Will there be a religious service at the home of the bereaved?

No.

Will food be served?

Possibly, but no alcoholic beverages.

How soon after the funeral will a mourner usually return to a normal work schedule?

A few days, depending upon individual preference. The Church has no set tradition.

How soon after the funeral will a mourner usually return to a normal social schedule?

This is entirely the choice of the bereaved, since the Church has no set tradition. It is often determined by local cultural traditions.

Are there mourning customs to which a friend who is not a member of the Pentecostal Church of God should be sensitive?

No.

Are there rituals for observing the anniversary of the death?

No.

29

Presbyterian

HISTORY AND BELIEFS

The Presbyterian Church was founded on the ideals of the Protestant Reformation and based on the concept of democratic rule under the authority of God. John Calvin (1509-1564) is the father of Presbyterianism.

All Presbyterians are required to trust in Christ as their forgiving savior, promise to follow Christ and His example for living, and commit themselves to attend church and to become involved in its work. They believe in the Holy Spirit (the empowering presence of God) speaking through the Bible, and in the sanctity of life.

Presbyterian theology emphasizes the majesty of God, who is conceived not just as truth or beauty, but also as intention, purpose, energy and will. The human counterpart of this is understanding the Christian life as the embodiment of the purposes of God and the working out of these purposes in one's life. Because of this, Presbyterians include many social activists, and those who try to shape and influence culture and history.

The Presbyterian Church (USA) was formed when the Presbyterian Church in the United States merged in 1983 with the United Presbyterian Church in the United States of America. The consolidation ended a schism that occurred during the Civil War when Southern Presbyterians broke away from the Presbyterian Church in the United States of America to create the Presbyterian Church in the Confederate States. Today's Presbyterian Church is the result of at least 10 different denominational mergers over the last 250 years and is strongly ecumenical in outlook.

The Presbyterian Church in Canada was formed in 1875 by the union of four branches of Presbyterianism that had been established as Europeans settled the country. The church experienced remarkable growth during the next 50 years, reaching almost 1.5 million members, the largest church in the country of 8.7 million people. Presbyterians had initiated discussions with the Methodist and Congregationalist churches, leading to the formation of the United Church of Canada in 1925. But a third of Presbyterians were not satisfied with the final plans and stayed out of the new denomination.

U. S. churches: 11,328
U. S. membership: 3.6 million
(data from the 1998 Yearbook of American and Canadian Churches*)*

Canadian churches: 1,010
Canadian membership: 145,328
(data from the 1998 Yearbook of American and Canadian Churches*)*

FUNERALS AND MOURNING

Presbyterians believe that in heaven the souls of the faithful are reunited with God in a warm and loving relationship. They also believe that it is not for humans to judge the fate of the unfaithful.

The funeral follows the order for Sunday worship, with prayers added for both the deceased and for oneself. Scripture texts that are used convey assurances of eternal life. The funeral usually lasts about 30 to 60 minutes.

BEFORE THE CEREMONY

How soon after the death does the funeral usually take place?
Usually within two to three days.

What should a non-Presbyterian do upon hearing of the death of a member of that faith?
Telephone the bereaved to offer your condolences. Whether one visits the home of the bereaved varies with the mourners' preference and predisposition. Those who are known to be more "open" would probably welcome visitors. Those who are more private might prefer no visitors. One can certainly call the bereaved to get a sense of their preference.

APPROPRIATE ATTIRE

Men: Jacket and tie. No head covering is required.

Women: Dresses or skirt and blouse. Open-toed shoes and modest jewelry permitted. Hems need not reach the knees nor must arms be covered. No head covering is required.

There are no rules regarding colors of clothing, but dark, somber colors are recommended.

GIFTS

Is it appropriate to send flowers or make a contribution?
Flowers are appreciated. They may be sent to the bereaved or to the funeral home before the funeral upon hearing the news of the death or shortly thereafter. Other contributions are not customary, although the family may suggest contributions to charity in lieu of flowers.

Is it appropriate to send food?
Yes, to the home of the bereaved after the funeral.

THE CEREMONY

Where will the ceremony take place?
At a church or a funeral home.

When should guests arrive and where should they sit?
Arrive on time. Sit wherever you wish.

If arriving late, are there times when a guest should *not* enter the ceremony?
If you arrive late, wait to be seated.

Will the bereaved family be present at the church or the funeral home before the ceremony?
It is not customary for the family to be publicly present before the service.

Is there a traditional greeting for the family?
Just offer your condolences.

Will there be an open casket?
Rarely.

Is a guest expected to view the body?
This is the individual's choice to make.

What is appropriate behavior upon viewing the body?
Silent prayer.

Who are the major officiants at the ceremony and what do they do?
▪ *The pastor or minister*, who officiates.

What books are used?

In the U.S., the two main books in the service are a hymnal and a Bible. Since there are no prescribed editions of either, hymnals and the version of the Bible may differ from one congregation to another. The most recent edition of the Old and New Testaments recommended for Presbyterians is the New Revised Standard Version, which is printed by several publishers. The most recent hymnal is the *Presbyterian Hymnal* (Louisville, Ky.: Westminster/John Knox Press, 1990). No individual Presbyterian or individual Presbyterian church is required to use these.

In Canada, the two main books in worship are *The Book of Praise* and the Bible. *The Book of Praise* contains the hymns sung by the congregation. There is also growing use of a Psalter (1997) that allows for the Psalms to be read or (in very few churches) chanted.

To indicate the order of the ceremony:

A program or bulletin will be distributed and the pastor or minister will announce the service.

Will a guest who is not a Presbyterian be expected to do anything other than sit?

Guests are not expected to do or say anything at the funeral.

Are there any parts of the ceremony in which a guest who is not a Presbyterian should *not* participate?

No.

If not disruptive to the ceremony, is it okay to:
◘ **Take pictures?** No.
◘ **Use a flash?** No.
◘ **Use a video camera?** No.
◘ **Use a tape recorder?** No.

Will contributions to the church be collected at the ceremony?

No.

THE INTERMENT

Should guests attend the interment?

Yes.

Whom should one ask for directions?

The ushers.

What happens at the graveside?

The officiating pastor or minister recites prayers. The graveside service may last 10 to 15 minutes.

Do guests who are not Presbyterians participate at the graveside service?

No. They are simply present.

COMFORTING THE BEREAVED

Is it appropriate to visit the home of the bereaved after the funeral?

This depends on the preferences of the bereaved. There is no set tradition. Frequently, mourners welcome visitors at their home after the funeral. This imparts a sense of community to the grieving process. Other mourners may prefer solitude and privacy.

Will there be a religious service at the home of the bereaved?

No.

Will food be served?

Possibly. This is at the discretion of the hosts.

How soon after the funeral will a mourner usually return to a normal work schedule?

This is left to the discretion of the mourner, but is usually about a week.

How soon after the funeral will a mourner usually return to a normal social schedule?

This is left to the discretion of the mourner, but is usually about a week.

Are there mourning customs to which a friend who is not Presbyterian should be sensitive?

No.

Are there rituals for observing the anniversary of the death?

No.

30

Quaker
(Religious Society of Friends)

HISTORY AND BELIEFS

The name *Quaker* was originally a nickname for the Children of Light or the Friends of Truth, as they called themselves. Members of the group were said to tremble or quake with religious zeal, and the nickname stuck. In time, they came to be known simply as "Friends."

The central Quaker conviction is that the saving knowledge and power of God are present as divine influences in each person through what has been variously called the "inner light," the "light of the eternal Christ within" or "the Seed within." Many affirm their acceptance of Jesus as their personal savior. Others conceive of the inward guide as a universal spirit that was in Jesus in abundant nature and is in everyone to some degree.

This reliance on the Spirit within was a direct challenge to religions that relied on outward authority, such as Catholicism or mainstream Protestantism. Largely because of this, Quakers were persecuted from the time they were founded in England in the 1650s. This tapered off about four decades later, and the English Quakers continued to grow and establish Quaker meetings, or congregations, in many parts of the world, especially in the British colonies in North America.

Quakers do not have ordained ministers and do not celebrate outward Christian sacraments. They seek, instead, an inward reality and contend that all life is sacramental.

Belief in the "inner light" present in every person also accounts for the distinctive nature of unprogrammed Quaker worship, in which the congregation is silent except when individuals are moved to speak. This conviction also motivates Quaker confidence in working for the kingdom of God in this world and their emphasis over the years on nonviolence and peace, abolishing slavery, relieving suffering, improving housing, educational and employment opportunities, reforming prisons and eliminating prejudice and discrimination against minorities and the underprivileged.

Quakers are strongly opposed to war and conscription and seek to remove the causes of war and conflict. While a few Quakers have accepted the draft and fought in wars, most declare themselves to be conscientious objectors. A small minority are draft resisters, and refuse to register or in any way cooperate with the military system.

U.S. meetings or congregations: 1,200
U.S. membership: 104,000
(data from the 1998 Yearbook of American and Canadian Churches)

Canadian meetings or worship groups: 57
Canadian membership: 1,126
(data from Reports, Ottawa: Canadian Yearly Meeting, 1998)

FUNERALS AND MOURNING

There are many Quaker attitudes about the possibility of life after death, since the Society of Friends is a religious body without creeds. Friends' beliefs about afterlife can be divided into three main areas:

- There is no individual survival, but the good (and possibly the evil, also) that we do lives on in the lives of those who come after us.
- The human spirit survives. This belief is not linked to the traditional duality of heaven or hell or to any theory of redemption by a savior figure. Instead, it sees survival after death as a continuation of this life, but with the possibility of progressing from one stage to another. Some Quakers also believe in rebirth or reincarnation.
- An approach closer to the traditional Christian belief which accepts heaven and hell as places where souls go after the death of the physical body. One's destiny depends on the life led while on earth.

A Quaker funeral, or memorial meeting, is either "unprogrammed" or "programmed." Unprogrammed meetings are held in the traditional manner of the Friends on the basis of silence. Worshippers sit and wait for divine guidance and inspiration. If so moved, they then speak to the group. This is called "vocal ministry."

Programmed meetings are planned in advance and usually include hymn singing, vocal prayers, Bible reading, silent worship and a sermon.

In many cases, worship is led by a pastor, who is generally paid and is responsible for some other pastoral services in the meeting.

Either form of meeting usually lasts an hour.

BEFORE THE CEREMONY

How soon after death does the funeral usually take place?
This varies with the individual family. Scheduling the memorial service or meeting mostly depends on its convenience to the most people since it is independent of the actual burial, which may take place within two to three days after death.

What should a non-Quaker do upon hearing of the death of a member of that faith?
Telephone, visit or send letters of sympathy to the bereaved. There is no specific "ritual" for calling or expressing sympathy to someone who is mourning.

APPROPRIATE ATTIRE

Men: Jacket and tie. No head covering is required.

Women: A dress or a skirt and blouse. Clothing should be modest. Open-toed shoes and modest jewelry are permissible. No head covering is required.

There are no rules regarding colors of clothing, but dark, somber colors are recommended.

GIFTS

Is it appropriate to send flowers or make a contribution?
Both are appropriate. Frequently, obituary notices in local newspapers will list specific charities to which contributions can be made in memory of the deceased.

Is it appropriate to send food?
Close friends and neighbors may bring food to the home of the bereaved.

THE CEREMONY

Where will the ceremony take place?
Usually in a Quaker meetinghouse, sometimes in a funeral home, and very rarely in a home.

When should guests arrive and where should they sit?
Arrive early. Usually ushers will advise guests on where to sit.

If arriving late, are there times when a guest should *not* enter the ceremony?
Do not enter when anyone is speaking.

Are there times when a guest should *not* leave the ceremony?
It is inappropriate to leave, especially when anyone is speaking.

Will the bereaved family be present at the meetinghouse or funeral home before the ceremony?
No.

Is there a traditional greeting for the family?
No.

Will there be an open casket?
Very rarely.

Is a guest expected to view the body?
This is entirely optional.

What is appropriate behavior upon viewing the body?
Silence.

Who are the major officiants at the ceremony and what do they do?
A person appointed by a meeting's Oversight Committee may explain Quaker custom at a memorial meeting to the non-Quakers present. This person may close the meeting at the appropriate time with a handshake to those seated nearby.

What books are used?
The Bible or a hymnal.

To indicate the order of the ceremony:
A program may be distributed that includes an obituary.

Will a guest who is not a Quaker be expected to do anything other than sit?
No, especially since most Quakers simply sit during the service unless they are moved to speak or offer a prayer or message that comes out of the silence. All present, Quaker and non-Quaker, are welcome to speak if moved to do so.

Are there any parts of the ceremony in which a guest who is not a Quaker should *not* participate?
No.

If not disruptive to the ceremony, is it okay to:
▪ **Take pictures?** No.
▪ **Use a flash?** No.
▪ **Use a video camera?** No.
▪ **Use a tape recorder?** Yes. This is often done, but it is still important to get permission from the family.

Will contributions to the meeting be collected at the ceremony?
No.

THE INTERMENT

Should guests attend the interment?
No. Usually only close family members attend.

Whom should one ask for directions?
See above.

What happens at the graveside?
The body is committed to the ground. If there has been a cremation, the ashes are either buried or put in a vault. Sometimes, the ashes are scattered.

Do guests who are not Quakers participate at the graveside ceremony?
No. They are simply present.

COMFORTING THE BEREAVED

Is it appropriate to visit the home of the bereaved after the funeral?
Yes, although there is no specific "ritual" for calling or expressing sympathy to someone who is mourning. Nor is there a "ritual" that guides the behavior of the mourners.

Will there be a religious service at the home of the bereaved?
No.

Will food be served?
Possibly.

How soon after the funeral will a mourner usually return to a normal work schedule?

This varies according to one's personal needs. There is no doctrine on mourning.

How soon after the funeral will a mourner usually return to a normal social schedule?

This varies according to one's personal needs. The Quaker emphasis is to resume the fabric of one's life.

Are there rituals for observing the anniversary of the death?

No.

31

Reformed Church in America/Canada

HISTORY AND BELIEFS

The Reformed Church began in the 1500s in Europe when groups of Christians who were opposed to any authority or practice that they believed could not be supported by a careful study of the Bible set themselves apart from the established Roman Church of the time. These Reformers adhered to the basic teachings of the early Christian church, but they also wrote new teachings, such as the Heidelberg Catechism, which was first published in 1563 and is still a standard that guides the life and religious witness of the Reformed Church in America.

The tone of the Heidelberg Catechism is mild, gentle and devotional, and celebrates the comfort that one can derive in life and in death from Jesus Christ. The Reformed Church in America requires every minister to cover the contents of the Heidelberg Catechism once every four years in his or her preaching.

The Reform movement's first church in America was the Reformed Dutch Church, which was founded in 1628 in New Amsterdam (now New York City). Not until 1764 was there a Reformed Church in the British colonies that used the English language. Starting with the American Revolution, the Dutch influence in the Church waned as the number of congregants of Scottish, German and English extraction increased. Finally, in 1867, the Church changed its name to the Reformed Church in America.

The Canadian branch of the denomination, which consists of 41 churches, is called the Reformed Church in Canada. (The Reform tradition is also represented in Canada by the Christian Reformed Church of North

184

America, which has 244 churches, a membership of 47,000 and offices in Burlington, Ontario.)

Each of the Reformed Church's local congregations is governed by a "consistory," which is comprised of the church's pastor and elected elders and deacons. Each church belongs to a "classis," which oversees the congregations within its particular jurisdiction. Each classis sends representatives to its regional synod, of which there are seven in the United States and one in Canada. It also sends representatives to the General Synod, which meets annually to set direction and policy for the Church as a whole.

The Church now supports missionaries on five continents. While the Church has been making concerted outreach to non-whites in the United States in recent years, its membership is still predominantly people with an Anglo-Saxon heritage: 95 percent of Church members are Caucasian; four percent are African-American; and two percent are Asian, Native American or Hispanic.

U.S. and Canadian churches: 950
U.S. and Canadian membership: 310,603
(*data from the* 1998 Yearbook of American and Canadian Churches)

FUNERALS AND MOURNING

In the Reformed Church, a funeral service is a time of comfort and hope for the bereaved. The hope of Church members is summarized by Jesus' words from John 11:25-26, "I am the resurrection and the life, says the Lord; whoever believes in Me though he die, yet shall he live; and whoever lives and believes in Me shall never die."

The Reformed Church believes that to be absent from the body is to be present with the Lord.

The funeral is a service in itself. It lasts about 20 to 30 minutes.

BEFORE THE CEREMONY

How soon after the death does the funeral usually take place?

Two to three days.

What should someone who is not a member of the Reformed Church do upon hearing of the death of a member of that faith?

Telephone or visit the bereaved family or send a card to the bereaved to express your condolences.

APPROPRIATE ATTIRE

Men: A jacket and tie. No head covering is required.

Women: A dress or a skirt and blouse. Clothing need not cover the arms and hems need not reach below the knees. Open-toed shoes and modest jewelry are permissible. No head covering is required.

Dark, somber colors of clothing are advised. Bright, flashy tones are strongly discouraged.

GIFTS

Is it appropriate to send flowers or make a contribution?

Flowers may be sent to the home of the bereaved upon hearing of the death or after the funeral, or they may be sent to the church or funeral home where the funeral ceremony will be held. Contributions to a church or organization designated by the family may be made after the funeral.

Is it appropriate to send food?

Yes. This may be sent to the home of the bereaved.

THE CEREMONY

Where will the ceremony take place?

Either in a church or a funeral home.

When should guests arrive and where should they sit?

Arrive a few minutes before the time for which the ceremony has been scheduled. Sit wherever you wish, unless a specially marked section has been reserved for immediate family.

If arriving late, are there times when a guest should *not* enter the ceremony?

Do not enter during prayers, the sermon or the eulogy. Follow ushers' guidance about entering the ceremony.

Will the bereaved family be present at the church or funeral home before the ceremony?

Sometimes.

Is there a traditional greeting for the family?

No. Just offer your condolences.

Will there be an open casket?

Rarely. This depends on local customs and the preference of the family. "Viewing" time is sometimes scheduled in the days or hours before the funeral. "Viewing" may also be offered during or at the end of the funeral service itself.

Is a guest expected to view the body?

This is entirely optional. If there is a "viewing" at the funeral and you do not wish to participate, excuse yourself from the line that forms to pass the casket. If you happen to be in the line that passes the casket and you do not wish to view the body, simply avert your eyes.

What is appropriate behavior upon viewing the body?

View it silently and somberly. Do not touch it or place any flowers or memorabilia in the casket.

Who are the major officiants at the ceremony and what do they do?

- *A pastor,* who officiates and delivers the sermon.
- *Possibly a family member or a close friend,* who may also deliver a eulogy.

What books are used?

No books are used by the bereaved or guests.

To indicate the order of the ceremony:

Usually a program will be distributed; sometimes the pastor will make periodic announcements.

Will a guest who is not a member of the Reformed Church be expected to do anything other than sit?

No. It is entirely optional for guests to read prayers aloud or to sing, stand or kneel when those present do so. In most funerals officiated by the Reformed Church, congregants do not kneel. In those churches where kneeling occurs, those guests who do not kneel should remain seated.

Are there any parts of the ceremony in which a guest who is not a member of the Reformed Church should *not* participate?

No.

If not disruptive to the ceremony, is it okay to:

- Take pictures? No.
- Use a flash? No.
- Use a video camera? No.
- Use a tape recorder? No.

Will contributions to the church be collected at the ceremony?

No.

THE INTERMENT

Should guests attend the interment?

This is entirely optional and is usually at the discretion of the guest, unless the minister announces at the funeral ceremony that the interment is only for family members.

Whom should one ask for directions?

The funeral director.

What happens at the graveside?

Scriptures are read, prayers are recited and the casket is placed in the ground.

Do guests who are not members of the Reformed Church participate at the graveside ceremony?

No, they are simply present.

COMFORTING THE BEREAVED

Is it appropriate to visit the home of the bereaved after the funeral?

Often, there is a reception at the church or home of the bereaved after the funeral. If not, visiting a few days after the funeral is appropriate. It is recommended that the length of the visit be fairly brief, such as 15 to 20 minutes.

Will there be a religious service at the home of the bereaved?

Seldom is this done.

Will food be served?

No.

How soon after the funeral will a mourner usually return to a normal social schedule?

The Reformed Church does not specify the number of days that one should formally be in mourning. Local, ethnic and cultural customs are more relevant that any particular religious tradition of the Church.

Are there mourning customs to which a friend who is not a member of the Reformed Church should be sensitive?

No. Local, ethnic and cultural customs are more relevant that any particular religious tradition of the Church.

Are there rituals for observing the anniversary of the death?

No. Local, ethnic and cultural customs are more relevant that any particular religious tradition of the Church.

32

Roman Catholic

HISTORY AND BELIEFS

The term "catholic" was first applied around 100 A.D. to the Christian Church, which was then one entity. It meant being geographically universal, continuous with the Christian past and transcending language, race and nation. The test of catholicity was communion with the universal Church and with the See of Rome.

After the eastern and western wings of the church divided in 1054 A.D., "catholic" was more usually used to refer to the church in the west under the spiritual leadership of the Holy See based in Rome. (This is commonly known as the Vatican.) Since the 16th century, "Roman Catholic" has meant the religious body which acknowledges the pope's authority and the Vatican as the center of ecclesiastical unity.

In the 19th century, the church became increasingly centralized in Rome. In 1870, Vatican Council I declared that the pope has jurisdictional primacy over the entire church, and that under certain circumstances, he is infallible in proclaiming doctrines of faith and morals.

In Roman Catholic teaching, revelation is summed up in Jesus Christ, who commanded his apostles to teach the gospel. To preserve the living gospel, the apostles appointed bishops as their successors. Roman Catholics believe in the unity of God, who is understood as God the Father, God the Son (Jesus Christ) and God the Holy Spirit. Catholicism teaches that original sin—Adam and Eve's expulsion from the Garden of Eden for disobeying God—alienated humanity from God, but did not totally corrupt man and woman, and that grace can fully make a sinner just.

Catholics especially venerate Mary, the mother of Jesus. Catholics believe that Mary was conceived without original sin, and that she was a virgin when Jesus was conceived.

Roman Catholicism has about 900 million members in 2,000 dioceses around the world.

U.S. churches: 22,728
U.S. membership: 61.2 million
(data from the 1998 Yearbook of American and Canadian Churches*)*

Canadian churches: 5,706
Canadian membership: 12.5 million
(data from the 1998 Yearbook of American and Canadian Churches*)*

FUNERALS AND MOURNING

Roman Catholicism deeply believes in immortality. Each human does not face utter spiritual dissolution since God loves him or her. Not only does all love desire immortality, but God's love *is* immortality. On the "last day" when the Messiah has arrived, one's physical body joins the spirit in the beatific vision of heaven or the damnation of hell.

A Catholic funeral may be part of a larger service or a ceremony in itself. If it is part of another service, that will be a mass. (For details on the mass, see "The Basic Service" section above.)

The first day after a death is usually reserved for the family to make arrangements for the funeral. The second day is often reserved for a wake, which may last for possibly one to two days. It is most commonly held at the funeral home. The style of wake varies (i.e., food, beverages, mood, prayer) widely and usually depends on the ethnicity of the deceased and his or her family. However, common to all wakes is an opportunity for community, friends and relatives to gather, pray and express their sympathies to the family of the deceased, to whom they also pay their respects.

BEFORE THE CEREMONY

How soon after the death does the funeral usually take place?
Usually within two to three days. Sometimes as much as one week later.

What should a non-Catholic do upon hearing of the death of a member of that faith?
Telephone the bereaved at home or visit them at the funeral home to express condolences.

APPROPRIATE ATTIRE

Men: Jacket and tie. No head covering required.

Women: Dress or a skirt and blouse or a pants suit. Jewelry and open-toed shoes are acceptable. Clothing should be modest, depending on the fashion and the locale. No head covering required.

Black or equally sober colors are recommended.

GIFTS

Is it appropriate to send flowers or make a contribution?
Flowers of any kind are appreciated. They may be sent upon hearing the news of the death or shortly thereafter. They may be sent to the home of the deceased before or after the funeral or to the funeral home before the funeral.

   Contributions are not customary unless the family indicates they are appropriate.

Is it appropriate to send food?
Yes, to the home of the bereaved before or after the funeral.

THE CEREMONY

Where will the ceremony take place?
At a church or a funeral home.

When should guests arrive and where should they sit?
Arrive on time. Sit wherever you like.

If arriving late, are there times when a guest should *not* enter the ceremony?
No.

Will the bereaved family be present at the church or funeral home before the ceremony?
Yes.

Is there a traditional greeting for the family?
Offer your condolences.

Will there be an open casket?
Usually.

Is a guest expected to view the body?
Yes.

What is appropriate behavior upon viewing the body?
Silent prayer.

Who are the major officiants at the ceremony and what do they do?
◼ The priest, who says the mass and the prayers at graveside.

What books are used?
The hymnal, the New American Bible (or another authorized translation), and a prayer book, which is also called a missal.

To indicate the order of the ceremony:
A program will be distributed.

Will a guest who is not a Catholic be expected to do anything other than sit?
Guests are expected to stand with the other mourners. It is optional for them to kneel, read prayers aloud and sing with the congregation.

Are there any parts of the ceremony in which a non-Catholic guest should *not* participate?
Such guests should not receive communion or say any prayers contradictory to the beliefs of their own faith.

If not disruptive to the ceremony, is it okay to:
◼ **Take pictures?** No. Verify beforehand with the priest or usher.
◼ **Use a flash?** No. Verify beforehand with the priest or usher.
◼ **Use a video camera?** No. Verify beforehand with the priest or usher.
◼ **Use a tape recorder?** No. Verify beforehand with the priest or usher.

Will contributions to the church be collected at the ceremony?
No.

THE INTERMENT

Should guests attend the interment?
Yes.

Whom should one ask for directions?
The funeral director.

What happens at the graveside?
The priest leads prayers for the deceased.

Do guests who are not Catholics participate at the graveside ceremony?
No. They are simply present.

COMFORTING THE BEREAVED

Is it appropriate to visit the home of the bereaved after the funeral?

Yes, briefly.

Will there be a religious service at the home of the bereaved?

No.

Will food be served?

Possibly. Given the broad ethnic mixture of Catholicism, some Catholics may have a "wake," at which food (and often, drink) is served.

How soon after the funeral will a mourner usually return to a normal work schedule?

Perhaps a week.

How soon after the funeral will a mourner usually return to a normal social schedule?

Perhaps a week.

Are there mourning customs to which a friend who is not a Catholic should be sensitive?

No.

Are there rituals for observing the anniversary of the death?

There is a mass on the annual anniversary of the death.

33

Seventh-day Adventist

HISTORY AND BELIEFS

The Seventh-day Adventist Church stemmed from a worldwide religious revival in the mid-1800s when people of many faiths fervently believed biblical prophecies that they interpreted as meaning that Jesus Christ's second coming, or "advent," was imminent.

When Christ did not come in the 1840s, a group of these disappointed Adventists in the U.S. concluded that they had misinterpreted prophetic events, and that the second coming was still in the future. This same group later became known as Seventh-day Adventists, which organized formally as a denomination in 1863.

Adventists anticipate and prepare for the world's end in conjunction with the second coming of Jesus Christ. They believe that the end of the world is near and that eternal hell for the wicked is not consistent with the concept of a "loving Father." Instead, they believe in eventual annihilation of the wicked and eternal bliss for the saved. After a thousand-year reign of the saints with Christ in Heaven, the wicked will be raised and, along with Satan, annihilated. Out of the chaos of the old earth will emerge a new earth, which the redeemed will inherit as their everlasting home.

Worldwide, there are about eight million Seventh-day Adventists. The movement grows by about seven percent annually and has more than 37,000 congregations in over 200 countries.

In addition to a mission program, the church has the largest worldwide Protestant parochial school system with over 800,000 elementary through college students in more than 5,400 schools. It also operates medical schools and hospitals.

U.S. churches: 4,363
U.S. membership: 809,000
(data from the 1998 Yearbook of American and Canadian Churches*)*

Canadian churches: 336
Canadian membership: 46,961
(data from 1997)

FUNERALS AND MOURNING

Seventh-day Adventists believe that the deceased sleep until the resurrection of Jesus. A Seventh-day Adventist funeral usually lasts about 15 to 30 minutes.

BEFORE THE CEREMONY

How soon after the death does the funeral usually take place?
Within one week of the death.

What should someone who is not a Seventh-day Adventist do upon hearing of the death of a member of that faith?
Telephone or visit to express sorrow. Express such words of comfort as "I sense your grief and share it with you." When speaking with each other, Adventists usually follow this phrase with, "We look for the coming resurrection." One should not consign the deceased to heaven or hell.

APPROPRIATE ATTIRE

Men: Jacket and tie. No head covering required.

Women: Dress or a skirt and blouse. No head covering required. Clothing should cover the arms, and hems should be below the knee.

No jewelry should be worn.

Somber colors are recommended.

GIFTS

Is it appropriate to send flowers or make a contribution?
It is not appropriate to make a donation, but it is appropriate to send flowers to the funeral or to the deceased's home before or after the funeral. The bereaved can also be helped by offering to transport incoming relatives from airports or bus or train stations or offering to help with errands.

Is it appropriate to send food?

It is appropriate to bring food after the funeral to the home of the deceased or to the place of a memorial meal, which could be elsewhere.

THE CEREMONY

Where will the ceremony take place?

Either in a church or funeral home.

When should guests arrive and where should they sit?

It is customary to arrive early. If there is no usher, sit in any seat.

If arriving late, are there times when a guest should *not* enter the ceremony?

Do not enter during prayer.

Will the bereaved family be present at the church or funeral home before the ceremony?

Often.

Is there a traditional greeting for the family?

It is appropriate to offer the family a brief word of encouragement before the funeral.

Will there be an open casket?

Usually.

Is a guest expected to view the body?

This is optional.

What is appropriate behavior upon viewing the body?

Simply stand in silent observation.

Who are the major officiants at the ceremony and what do they do?

■ *A clergyman,* who leads the service; possibly also an associate clergy or layperson; musician(s).

What books are used?

The clergy alone uses the Bible.

To indicate the order of the ceremony:

A program will be distributed.

Will a guest who is not a Seventh-day Adventist be expected to do anything other than sit?

You are not expected to do anything other than sit respectfully.

Are there any parts of the ceremony in which a guest who is not a Seventh-day Adventist should *not* participate?
No.

If not disruptive to the service, is it okay to:
◾ **Take pictures?** No.
◾ **Use a flash?** No.
◾ **Use a video camera?** No.
◾ **Use a tape recorder?** No.

Will contributions to the church be collected at the ceremony?
No.

THE INTERMENT

Should guests attend the interment?
This is optional.

Whom should one ask for directions?
The funeral director.

What happens at the the graveside?
There will be a brief message of encouragement and prayer from the clergyman.

Do guests who are not Seventh-day Adventists participate at the graveside ceremony?
No. They are simply present.

COMFORTING THE BEREAVED

Is it appropriate to visit the home of the bereaved after the funeral?
Yes, especially during the first few days after the funeral. More than once is appropriate. One should visit briefly, perhaps ten minutes, to express words of encouragement or to offer to help with any difficulties the bereaved may encounter.

Will there be a religious service at the home of the bereaved?
There are no special customs or religious services at the home.

Will food be served?
No.

How soon after the funeral will a mourner usually return to a normal work schedule?

This is left entirely to the discretion of individual mourners since the Bible does not mandate specific periods for mourning. Probably within days of the funeral.

How soon after the funeral will a mourner usually return to a normal social schedule?

Probably within days of the funeral.

Are there rituals for observing the anniversary of the death?

No, since the Bible does not mandate such rituals.

34

Sikh

HISTORY AND BELIEFS

The Sikh faith originated in India in the late 15th century through the life and teachings of Guru Nanak (1469–1539 C.E.), the first Sikh guru. At a time of great religious conflict, he taught that all creation is a part of the One Creator. After Guru Nanak's life, he passed his "light" on successively to nine other gurus who further evolved his teachings. Each guru denounced India's caste system and the oppression of anyone based on class, creed, color or sex.

The 10th and last human guru, Guru Gobind Singh, initiated his followers as the *Khalsa*, which means "the Pure Ones." He instructed the *Khalsa* not to cut their hair (since doing so would tamper with God's image, in which they were created); to dress in white Sikh attire called *bana*, which consists of turbans and dress-like garments called *kurtas* and leggings called *churidars*; to be monogamous; and to live righteously. Before dying in 1708, Guru Gobind Singh "gave" the guruship to the Sikh scriptures known as the *Siri Guru Granth Sahib*. These scriptures were compiled by the fifth guru, Arjan Dev, and contain sacred writings by some Sikh gurus and several Hindu and Moslem saints. Since then, Sikhs have bowed before the *Siri Guru Granth Sahib*, consulted it as their only guru and treated it with reverence.

Today, there are 20 million Sikhs throughout the world.

U.S. temples/*gurdwaras*: 260
U.S. membership: 305,000
(1996 data from Sikh Dharma International)

Canadian temples/*gurdwaras:* 100
Canadian membership: 300,000
(data from Sikh Society of Alberta, Edmonton, Alberta)

FUNERALS AND MOURNING

Sikhs believe in the cycle of reincarnation and that certain actions and attachments bind the soul to this cycle. The soul itself is not subject to death. Death is only the progression of the soul on its journey from God, through the created universe, and back to God again.

A Sikh tries to be constantly mindful of death so that he or she may be sufficiently prayerful, detached and righteous to break the cycle of birth and death and return to God. Because the soul never dies, there is no mourning at the death of a Sikh. All ceremonies commemorating a death include much prayer to help the soul be released from the bonds of reincarnation and to become one with God again.

After death, Sikhs prepare the body for the funeral with a yogurt bath while reciting prayers. Next the body is dressed in new clothes and the five symbols of a Sikh: *kesh,* or uncut hair; *kirpan,* the Sikh knife which represents compassion and one's task to defend the truth; *kara,* a stainless steel bracelet; *kachera,* special Sikh underwear; and *kanga,* a small comb.

A short ceremony takes place at the funeral home before the cremation. An *ardas,* or community prayer, is recited to begin the service. A minister may be present to offer prayers and say a few words, but this is optional. Two Sikh daily prayers, *Japji* and *Kirtan Sohila,* are recited, and the cremation begins. Although these prayers may be continuously recited throughout the cremation, the basic funeral service ends at this time, and guests may leave. This service usually lasts about 30 to 60 minutes.

Afterward, there may be another service at the *gurdwara,* but this is optional. Traditionally, the word *"akal,"* which means "undying," is chanted at this service to help release the soul to return to the Infinite. This second ceremony, which is a service in itself, lasts about one hour.

BEFORE THE CEREMONY

How soon after the death does the funeral usually take place?

The body of a Sikh is always cremated. This usually occurs within three days after death.

What should a non-Sikh do upon hearing of the death of a member of that faith?

It is fine to call the family of the deceased to express your love and concern and offer help or support they may need. In calling or writing, it is best not to focus on loss or sadness, but rather to help the family and friends remember the joy of the soul returning to its true Home with God.

APPROPRIATE ATTIRE

Men: A jacket and tie or more casual, modest clothing. Any color is fine. Shoes may be worn inside a funeral home, but not in a *gurdwara* service. The head should be covered with a hat, cap or scarf.

Women: A modest dress, a skirt and blouse, or a pants suit. It is best if the legs are covered enough to sit comfortably cross-legged. Shoes may be worn inside a funeral home, but not at a *gurdwara* service. The head should be covered with a scarf, hat or veil. Open-toed shoes (which may be worn only in the funeral home, *not* in the *gurdwara*) and modest jewelry are permissible.

There are no rules regarding colors of clothing.

GIFTS

Is it appropriate to send flowers or make a contribution?

Flowers, food or contributions to a charity chosen by the family of the deceased may be given, but are not expected.

Is it appropriate to send food?

Yes, but do not send food that contains meat, fish, eggs or alcohol.

THE CEREMONY

Where will the ceremony take place?

The pre-cremation ceremony will take place at a funeral home. The optional, post-cremation ceremony will be at the *gurdwara*.

When should guests arrive and where should they sit?

It is best to arrive early enough to be seated before the funeral service begins. At a funeral home, one may sit wherever one wishes, but the family of the deceased will sit in the front. For *gurdwara* services, everyone sits on the floor facing the *Siri Guru Granth Sahib*, the Sikh holy book, sometimes with the men on the left and women on the right.

If arriving late, are there times when a guest should *not* enter the ceremony?

One can enter the ceremony in the funeral home and quietly sit anywhere.

Wait at the entrance to the *gurdwara* until the *ardas*, or community prayer, ends and everyone has again been seated.

Will the bereaved family present at the funeral home before the ceremony?

Depending on the customs of a particular Sikh community, the body of the deceased may be displayed at a visitation before the funeral. If this is not the case, the family of the deceased will most likely arrive at the time of the ceremony and not before.

Is there a traditional greeting for the family?

Just offer your condolences.

Will there be an open casket?

Possibly, depending on the customs of a particular Sikh community.

Is a guest expected to view the body?

No.

What is appropriate behavior upon viewing the body?

Silently say a short prayer for the soul of the deceased as you pass by the casket.

Who are the major officiants at the ceremony and what do they do?

- *One person*, usually a close family member, officiates at the ceremony at the funeral home and leads the prayers recited there. Officiating at the service in the *gurdwara* are:
- *The Granthi or Giani Ji*, the person reading the *hukam* from the *Siri Guru Granth Sahib*. The *hukam*, which is a portion of the *Siri Guru Granth Sahib* chosen randomly by the reader, is first read in the original Gurmukhi language and then translated to English (or the main language of the congregation).
- *Attendants*, several people who sit behind the *Siri Guru Granth Sahib* and attend to it by frequently waving a long-handled brush made of long horse hair called a *chori sahib* above the *Siri Guru Granth Sahib* or who take out or put away the scriptures. The attendants also serve *prasad*, or sweet pudding, at the end of the service; read the *hukam* translation in English; and assist in the *gurdwara* in any way. Many people from the *sangat*, the congregation, participate in these functions.

◘ *Kirtanis,* musicians who lead the *sangat* in *kirtan,* songs of praise to God.

◘ *The master of ceremonies,* the person announcing guest speakers and the order of the service. This role is often fulfilled by the *gurdwara* secretary or *granthi.*

What books are used?

A *Nit Nem,* or daily prayer book of the Sikhs is used to recite the prayers before cremation. Since all prayers are read in Gurmukhi (the original language of the gurus), it is not expected for guests to also recite these. If desired, however, a *Nit Nam* with a transliteration may be available upon request.

To indicate the order of the ceremony:

In the funeral home, no one indicates the order of the ceremony that is held there. For the *gurdwara* service, there may be a written program and/or the Master of Ceremonies may make periodic announcements.

Will a guest who is not a Sikh be expected to do anything other than sit?

There are no expectations for guests attending the ceremony in the funeral home. Those guests attending the *gurdwara* ceremony will be expected to stand and sit at the same time as everyone else. It is entirely optional for guests to sing or bow to the *Siri Guru Granth Sahib,* although they are expected to accept *prasad* (sweet pudding), which is considered a blessing from the *Siri Guru Granth Sahib.* Customarily, one receives *prasad* with both hands together, palms up. One does not have to be a Sikh to eat the *prasad.*

Are there any parts of the ceremony in which a guest who is not a Sikh should *not* participate?

Guests may participate in all aspects of the ceremony in the funeral home. In the *gurdwara* ceremony, only Sikhs will be asked to serve *prasad,* read from the *Siri Guru Granth Sahib,* do the *ardas* (prayer) and to serve in any way needed. Other than this, guests may participate in every part of the *gurdwara* ceremony as desired.

If not disruptive to the ceremony, is it okay to:

◘ **Take pictures?** Only with prior permission of the family of the deceased and if intended solely for personal use.

◘ **Use a flash?** Only with prior permission of the family of the deceased and if intended solely for personal use.

◘ **Use a video camera?** Only with prior permission of the family of the deceased and if intended solely for personal use.

◾ **Use a tape recorder?** Only with prior permission of the family of the deceased and if intended solely for personal use.

Will contributions to the local Sikh temple be collected at the service?

No contributions will be collected at a funeral home service. At *gurdwara* services, money or flowers may be offered to the *Siri Guru Granth Sahib* at the time of bowing, but this is optional. Money may be placed in a box with a slot on it or on an offering plate. Either will be in front of the *Siri Guru Granth Sahib*. Other gifts may be placed in front of the *Siri Guru Granth Sahib*.

How much is customary to contribute?

The customary contribution is $1 to $5.

THE CREMATION

Should guests attend the cremation?

Usually only close family members remain for the cremation since it lasts several hours.

Whom should one ask for directions?

Friends or the family of the deceased.

What happens at the cremation?

An *ardas*, or community prayer, is recited to begin the service. A minister may offer prayers and say a few words, but this is optional. Two Sikh daily prayers, *Japji* and *Kirtan Sohila*, are recited, and the cremation begins.

Do guests who are not Sikhs participate at the cremation ceremony?

Not usually unless they are invited by the family to do so.

COMFORTING THE BEREAVED

Is it appropriate to visit the home of the bereaved after the funeral ceremony?

This is optional, though not really expected.

Will there be a religious service at the home of the bereaved?

Memorial services are often held at home, especially when the funeral ceremony has taken place in another city. Sometimes, the family of the deceased sponsors an *Akhand Path* (unbroken) or other reading of the *Siri*

Guru Granth Sahib. This may take place at their home, at the *gurdwara*, or elsewhere. During the *Akhand Path* service, the entire *Siri Guru Granth Sahib* is read in 48 hours in the Gurmukhi language or in 72 hours in English. People take turns reading the text.

Will food be served?

Possibly. Since Sikhs are prohibited from drinking alcoholic beverages, none will be offered.

How soon after the funeral will a mourner usually return to a normal work schedule?

Usually one returns to a normal work routine anywhere from a few days to a few weeks after the funeral. This is at the personal discretion of each individual.

How soon after the funeral will a mourner usually return to a normal social schedule?

Usually one returns to a normal social routine anywhere from a few days to a few weeks after the funeral. This is at the personal discretion of each individual.

Are there mourning customs to which a friend who is not a Sikh should be sensitive?

When visiting, it is best not to focus on loss or sadness, but rather to help the family and friends remember the joy of the soul returning to its true Home with God.

Are there rituals for observing the anniversary of the death?

No, although some Sikhs may choose to remember a deceased loved one in prayer during a *gurdwara* service on the anniversary of a death. Some Sikhs also choose to hold a special *gurdwara* and *langar* at the anniversary.

35

Unitarian Universalist

(also known as Unitarian or Universalist)

HISTORY AND BELIEFS

The Unitarian Universalist Association was created in 1961 when the American Unitarian Association and the Universalist Church of America merged. The purpose of the union was "to cherish and spread the universal truths taught by the great prophets and teachers of humanity in every age and tradition, immemorially summarized in the Judeo-Christian heritage as love to God and love to man."

The newly-formed Unitarian Universalist Association included both American and Canadian congregations. In the same year, 1961, the Canadian Unitarian Council was organized to provide services to Canadian congregations, which are members of both bodies.

Like its predecessors, the new denomination is committed to living in the tension between humanistic liberalism and Christianity, and prefers following reason, conscience and experience to following creeds. Unitarian Universalist churches make no official pronouncements on God, the Bible, Jesus, immortality or other theological questions that are often answered with finality by more traditional religions. Instead, Unitarian Universalism deems a religious way of life as being too important to be left to rigid creeds and dogmas, and there is frequent discussion among members and clergy about whether the faith has, indeed, grown beyond Judeo-Christianity and become something more universal. Unitarian Universalists reject the attitude that salvation is attainable only through the mediation of Jesus Christ and membership in a Christian Church. Thus, many believe that Unitarian Universalism is not a Christian faith today, although its historical and theological roots are undeniably Christian.

Unitarians trace their origins to a movement that began shortly after the death of Jesus Christ. According to present Unitarian teachings, many who personally knew Jesus rejected claims of his divinity. Instead, they focused on his humanity and his teachings, not on his alleged godliness. The movement was eventually named Arianism, after Arius, a priest from Alexandria who preached this belief. After the Council of Nicea adopted in 325 A.D. the concept of the Trinity—God, the Father; God, the Son; God, the Holy Ghost—those who embraced this idea denounced believers in God's unity as heretics.

Nevertheless, by the 16th century, Unitarian ideas had gained a foothold in Switzerland, Britain, Hungary and Italy. In 1683, the first Unitarian church to use that name was established in Transylvania. And by the first decade of the 19th century, 20 Unitarian churches had been established in England.

In the United States, Unitarianism got its impetus from the preaching and writings of William Ellery Channing in the early 19th century. Strongly concerned with liberal social causes, such as abolitionism and educational reform, the faith also gave birth to the Transcendentalism associated with Ralph Waldo Emerson and Henry David Thoreau.

While Unitarianism most often attracted the highly educated and intellectual, especially in New England, Universalism was initially an evangelistic, working-class movement with an uneducated clergy. Their "universalism" rested on a belief that all souls would eventually attain salvation. As with Unitarianism, it dates from the early days of Christianity, most notably the writings of Origen, an early Church father.

In the United States, circuit-rider ministers helped spread the faith so well that by the 1850s there were about 800,000 Universalists. By the 1900s, Universalism was the sixth largest denomination in the United States. After that, membership steadily declined, although its theological development eventually so paralleled that of Unitarianism that the two denominations could eventually merge.

In 19th-century Canada, Unitarian congregations were established in Montreal and Toronto, with the assistance of British Unitarians. Universalism entered Canada from the United States, and was largely centered in the Maritimes and Southern Ontario. Many Icelandic Lutherans in Manitoba were attracted to the more liberal Unitarian faith and established a number of congregations there. Unitarianism in Canada remained a very small faith group until the end of World War II, when there was a strong movement away from more traditional faiths, and new congregations and lay-led fellowships were established in many parts of the country.

Each local Unitarian Universalist congregation, which may be called a church, society or fellowship, adopts its own bylaws, elects its own officers and approves its budget. Each local congregation is affiliated with one of the 23 districts of the Unitarian Universalist Association of Congregations.

U.S. churches: 1,033
U.S. membership: 213,342
(1999 data from the Unitarian Universalist Association of Congregations)

Canadian churches: 44
Canadian membership: 5,038
(data from the Canadian Unitarian Council)

FUNERALS AND MOURNING

There is no specific Unitarian Universalist doctrine about afterlife. Some Unitarian Universalists believe in an afterlife; some doubt that there is one.

The Unitarian Universalist ritual that marks one's death is called a "memorial service," not a funeral.

The memorial service is a ceremony in itself and may last about 30 to 60 minutes. Some memorial services may last more than one hour.

BEFORE THE CEREMONY

How soon after the death does the memorial service usually take place?

Usually within one week; sometimes up to one month after the death. The length of time between the death and the memorial service is determined solely at the discretion of the family.

What should someone who is not a Unitarian Universalist do upon hearing of the death of a member of that faith?

Telephone or visit the bereaved to express your condolences and share your memories of the deceased. Such comments as "I am so very sorry for your loss" are appropriate. Such comments as "Now he/she is with God" or "It was God's will" are not appropriate.

APPROPRIATE ATTIRE

Men: A jacket and tie. No head covering is required.

Women: A dress. Hems need not reach below the knees nor must clothing cover the arms. Open-toed shoes and modest jewelry are permissible. No head covering is required.

Somber colors are recommended for clothing.

GIFTS

Is it appropriate to send flowers or make a contribution?

Flowers may be delivered to the home of the bereaved before the memorial service. Also, contributions ranging from $10 to $200 may be made to a fund or charity designated by the family or the deceased.

Is it appropriate to send food?

Yes. This may be sent to the home of the bereaved upon hearing of the death or after the memorial service.

THE CEREMONY

Where will the ceremony take place?

Usually in a funeral home; sometimes in a church.

When should guests arrive and where should they sit?

Arrive shortly before the time for which the memorial service has been called. Sit wherever you wish, except for the first two or three rows, which are usually reserved for the close family of the deceased.

If arriving late, are there times when a guest should *not* enter the ceremony?

No.

Will the bereaved family be present at the funeral home or church before the ceremony?

Sometimes.

Is there a traditional greeting for the family?

Express your condolences. Such comments as "I am so very sorry for your loss" are appropriate.

Will there be an open casket?

Rarely.

Is a guest expected to view the body?

Guests are not expected or obligated to view the body.

What is appropriate behavior upon viewing the body?

If one chooses to view the body, walk slowly and reverently past the casket.

Who are the major officiants at the ceremony and what do they do?

- *The minister,* who delivers a sermon and meditation and commits the body to the grave.
- *The eulogist,* who is chosen by the family of the deceased and delivers a eulogy in honor of the deceased.
- *The music director and organist,* who provide music.

What books are used?

A hymnal, *Singing the Living Tradition*, edited by the Hymnbook Resource Commission (Boston, Ma.: The Unitarian Universalist Association, 1993).

To indicate the order of the ceremony:

Usually either a program will be provided or a display near the front of the room where the memorial service is held will indicate the order.

Will a guest who is not a Unitarian Universalist be expected to do anything other than sit?

It is expected for guests to stand with congregants when they rise for songs or prayer. It is optional for guests to sing and read prayers aloud with congregants if this does not violate their own religious beliefs. There is no kneeling during a Unitarian Universalist memorial service.

Are there any parts of the ceremony in which a guest who is not a Unitarian Universalist should *not* participate?

No.

If not disruptive to the ceremony, is it okay to:

- **Take pictures?** No.
- **Use a flash?** No.
- **Use a video camera?** No.
- **Use a tape recorder?** Only with prior approval of the family of the deceased.

Will contributions to the church be collected at the ceremony?

No.

THE INTERMENT

Should guests attend the interment?

This is entirely optional.

Whom should one ask for directions?

The funeral director.

What happens at the graveside?

Prayers are recited and the body is committed to the ground.

Do guests who are not Unitarian Universalists participate at the graveside ceremony?

No. They are simply present.

COMFORTING THE BEREAVED

Is it appropriate to visit the home of the bereaved after the memorial service?

Yes. The length of the visit depends on one's relationship with the bereaved and with the deceased. When visiting, express your sympathy to the bereaved and offer specific help to them. Fond memories of the deceased are especially appreciated.

Will there be a religious service at the home of the bereaved?

No.

Will food be served?

Yes, possibly including alcoholic beverages.

How soon after the memorial service will a mourner usually return to a normal work schedule?

This is left to the discretion of the mourner, but is usually a few days to a few weeks.

How soon after the memorial service will a mourner usually return to a normal social schedule?

This is left to the discretion of the mourner, but is usually a few days to a few weeks.

Are there mourning customs to which a friend who is not a Unitarian Universalist should be sensitive?

No.

Are there rituals for observing the anniversary of the death?

No.

36

United Church of Canada

HISTORY AND BELIEFS

The United Church of Canada was created by an Act of Parliament in 1925 as a union of the country's Presbyterian, Methodist and Congregational denominations. In Western Canada, in communities unable to afford the luxury of separate churches, a number of informal Union churches had already formed, applying pressure on parent denominations to amalgamate.

Although Presbyterians provided the initial push for the three-denomination Union, in the end they also offered its greatest opposition; approximately one-third of Presbyterian congregations voted not to unite. The Methodist and Congregational denominations entered the Church Union as a whole.

The United Church sees itself as having a mandate to work toward further unions. In 1968, it was joined by the Evangelical United Brethren. A proposed union with the Anglican Church of Canada, however, foundered in the 1970s.

Its worship and policies are, inevitably, a product of its founding traditions. From the Methodists, the United Church inherited a passion for social justice; from the Presbyterians, a conciliar system for internal governance; from the Congregationalists, a stubborn refusal to be bound by arbitrary doctrine or dogma.

The United Church has been at the forefront of social change in Canada. It was the first mainline denomination in the world to ordain women as ministers. It welcomed draft dodgers during the Vietnam War, lobbied against alcohol and tobacco, urged recognition of the Republic of China, endorsed women's right to choice of abortion and, most recently, ruled that homosexuality is not, in and of itself, a bar to ordination.

The national court of the United Church is the General Council, which meets every three years. Only the General Council speaks for the United Church. Between Councils, elected officials of the church or various committees or divisions may interpret or comment on the Council's policies. Surprisingly, there are few doctrinal statements. The *Basis of Union* of 1925 contains *Twenty Articles of Faith,* developed as a statement of the common faith of the three founding denominations. The only *Statement of Faith* issued by the United Church itself came in 1940, with a teaching *Catechism* in 1942. In 1968, the General Council authorized a "New Creed" as an authentic expression of the United Church's faith. This "Creed" has since been revised twice, to eliminate exclusively masculine language, and to add concern for the natural environment.

The Congregationalist openness to diverse viewpoints means that ministers are required only to be in "essential agreement" with the *Twenty Articles.* As a result, the church's ministry encompasses a wide variety of theological viewpoints.

As a national denomination, the United Church has no branches or subsidiaries in any other country. It does have working partnerships with a number of other churches in other parts of the world. The United Church maintains membership in the world associations to which its predecessors belonged, such as the World Alliance of Reformed Churches.

Canadian churches: 3,872
Canadian membership: 720,000
(data from The United Church of Canada Yearbook *and the*
1998 Yearbook of American and Canadian Churches*)*

FUNERALS AND MOURNING

In the United Church of Canada, traditional funerals are often replaced by memorial services, which celebrate the life and faith of the departed person. Funerals, with a casket present, are increasingly rare. If a casket is present, it will more often be closed than open. More and more, United Church members choose cremation rather than burial.

Beliefs about life after death vary widely across the United Church of Canada. Some believe that after death they will be reunited with their loved ones. Others may believe that this life is all we have, and that death is final.

Officially, the United Church of Canada teaches that the resurrection of Jesus is symbolic of the resurrection that is possible for all who believe in him.

BEFORE THE CEREMONY

How soon after the death will the funeral usually take place?

Between a few days and a week. There are no religious requirements to have a funeral immediately. A memorial service may be held several weeks after a death, to allow time for mourners to gather from across the country.

What should someone who is not a member of the United Church do upon hearing of the death of a member of that church?

Telephone or visit the bereaved to offer sympathy. In some parts of the country, visits are made directly to the family's home. In others, visits are made at specified times to the funeral parlor. Check the obituary notice; if it makes no reference to visiting times at a funeral parlor, then visits may be made at any (reasonable) time in the home.

APPROPRIATE ATTIRE

Funerals call for more formality in dress than almost any other religious occasion in the United Church of Canada.

Men: Mainly suit and tie, dark colors preferred. In more casual cultures, slacks and sweaters may be acceptable.

Women: Dresses, dark colors, plain fabrics. Pants suits may be permissible, again, in darker colors. Arms and heads may be uncovered. Subdued jewelry is permissible.

GIFTS

Is it appropriate to send flowers or to make a contribution?

Check the obituary notice to see if the family wants to have donations made to a charity or cause in lieu of flowers.

If they accept flowers, the flowers should usually go to the church or funeral parlor rather than to the family home.

If donations are preferred, send them directly to the chosen charity, marked "In Memory of [name]." Some charities send notification of such gifts to the bereaved family; some don't. If you want the bereaved to know that you've made a donation, include a note providing their address so the charity will know where to send a notification.

Is it appropriate to send food?

Yes. Send or take it to the home of the bereaved.

THE CEREMONY

Where will the ceremony take place?

In a church or in a funeral parlor.

When should guests arrive and where should they sit?

Arrive early. Family and friends will be seated in a special block of reserved seats. Ushers will advise where to sit. If there are no ushers, guests may sit wherever they choose.

If arriving late, are there times when a guest should *not* enter the service?

Yes. Ushers will seat you when it is appropriate.

Will the bereaved family be present at the church or funeral home before the ceremony?

Possibly.

Is there a traditional greeting for the family?

No. Express sympathy. If time permits, invite the bereaved to talk about their feelings, and how they're coping with their loss. Share your favorite memories of the deceased person. Funny memories are just as acceptable as sorrowful ones.

Avoid preaching. Don't offer pat answers about the meaning of life or about God's promises of eternal life. Don't suggest that this is all God's will and will work out for the best in the end.

Will there be an open casket?

In the United Church, less and less often.

Is a guest expected to view the body?

This is optional, but if it is a memorial service, there will be no body to view.

What is appropriate behavior upon viewing the body?

Silence, or silent prayer.

Who are the major officiants at the ceremony and what do they do?

▪ *The minister(s)*, who will lead the service.

What books are used?

Voices United, the United Church's hymnbook (Etobicoke, Ont.: The United Church Publishing House, 1996). Most congregations also use *Songs for a Gospel People* (Winfield, B.C.: Wood Lake Books Inc., 1987), commonly referred to as "the green book." Many congregations provide Bibles, in one of the modern translations. A few provide the Psalms, most often in the *Good News* translation.

To indicate the order of the ceremony:
There will be a printed program or bulletin, and the minister will make announcements or give instructions.

Will a guest who is not a member of the United Church be expected to do anything other than sit?
Visitors are invited to participate along with the congregation in all aspects of a funeral or memorial service that do not violate their own personal beliefs.

Are there any parts of the ceremony in which a guest who is not a member of the United Church should *not* participate?
No.

If not disruptive to the service, is it okay to:
- **Take pictures?** No, unless you have received prior permission.
- **Use a flash?** No, unless you have received permission.
- **Use a video camera?** No, unless you have received prior permission.
- **Use a tape recorder?** Possibly, but ask first.

Will contributions to the church be collected at the ceremony?
No.

THE INTERMENT

With the increasing trend to cremation and memorial services, there may not be an interment. If there is, it may take place months later, as a private ceremony for the immediate family.

Should guests attend the interment?
This is optional. If it immediately follows a funeral service, probably yes. After a memorial service, no.

Whom should one ask for directions?
The funeral director.

What happens at the graveside?
If there is a formal interment or burial, of the casket or of ashes, you are simply expected to be present and to participate in the ceremony as you are able. The minister or presider will offer prayers. If responses are expected, they will either be familiar or will be printed in a program or bulletin. The casket or ashes will be lowered into the ground or placed in a vault. Guests may be invited to assist in sprinkling earth or sand; you are not obliged to participate if you do not wish to.

The rites of a fraternal order or of the military may be part of a graveside service.

Do guests who are not members of the United Church participate at the graveside ceremony?

Guests are invited to participate along with the congregation in all aspects of an interment or burial that do not violate their own personal beliefs.

COMFORTING THE BEREAVED

Is it appropriate to visit the home of the bereaved after the funeral?

Yes. At any mutually convenient time, and as often as you feel appropriate. Too often, families are expected to return to normal right after the ceremony. Grieving takes a lot longer than that. Visiting allows people to talk about their experience, turning painful memories into memories of painful memories.

How long you stay depends on your closeness to the bereaved. An average visit might be 15 to 30 minutes.

Will there be a religious service at the home of the bereaved?
No.

Will food be served?

Often, refreshments or a light meal will be served at a reception immediately following the memorial, funeral or interment service.

How soon after the funeral will a mourner usually return to a normal work schedule?

Depends on the person and the situation. There are no customs requiring a certain period of isolation, or a certain number of days off work. Most mourners will return to work within a week.

How soon after the funeral will a mourner usually return to a normal social schedule?

Depends on the person and the situation. Remember that grieving is a process. It can't, and shouldn't, be hurried.

Are there mourning customs to which a friend who is not a member of the United Church should be sensitive?
No.

Are there rituals for observing the anniversary of the death?
No.

37
United Church of Christ

HISTORY AND BELIEFS

Formed in 1957 by the merger of two churches, the United Church of Christ is one of the newer Protestant denominations in the United States.

The merger was between the Congregational Christian Churches, whose roots date back to 16th century England and to the Puritan and Separatist movements that settled New England; and the Evangelical and Reform Church, which had previously been formed by combining the German Reformed Church and the Evangelical Synod of North America.

According to the constitution of the United Church of Christ, Jesus Christ is the "sole Head" of the Church and each local congregation is its "basic unit." Local churches choose their own pastors and determine policy regarding membership, worship, budget and programs. Congregations cooperate in area groupings called "associations" and in larger regional bodies called "conferences." The General Synod, the Church's central deliberative body, meets biennially to conduct denominational business. More than half the Church's membership is in the New England and Midwestern states.

U.S. churches: 6,110
U.S. membership: 1.5 million
(data from the 1998 Yearbook of American and Canadian Churches*)*

FUNERALS AND MOURNING

A United Church of Christ funeral service, states the Church's *Book of Worship*, "recognizes both the pain and sorrow of the separation that accompanies death and the hope and joy of the promises of God to those who die and are raised in Jesus Christ. The service celebrates the life of the deceased, gives thanks for that person's life, and commends that life to God.... Its purpose is to affirm once more the powerful, steadfast love of God from which people cannot be separated, even by death."

The funeral service is almost always a service in itself. Ordinarily, it lasts about 15 to 30 minutes, although it may sometimes last up to 60 minutes.

BEFORE THE CEREMONY

How soon after the death does the funeral usually take place?
Within one week.

What should someone who is not a member of the United Church of Christ do upon hearing of the death of a member of that faith?
Telephone or visit the bereaved family or send a card to them to express your condolences.

APPROPRIATE ATTIRE

Men: A jacket and tie. No head covering is required.

Women: A dress or a skirt and blouse. Clothing need not cover the arms and hems need not reach below the knees. Open-toed shoes and modest jewelry are permissible. No head covering is required.

Dark, somber colors of clothing are advised. Bright, flashy tones are strongly discouraged.

GIFTS

Is it appropriate to send flowers or make a contribution?
Flowers may be sent to the home of the bereaved upon hearing of the death or after the funeral or they may be sent to the church or funeral home where the funeral service will be held. Contributions to a church or organization designated by the family may be made after the funeral.

Is it appropriate to send food?
Yes. This may be sent to the home of the bereaved.

THE CEREMONY

Where will the ceremony take place?
Either in a church or a funeral home.

When should guests arrive and where should they sit?

Arrive fifteen minutes before the time for which the service has been scheduled. Sit wherever you wish, unless a specially marked section has been reserved for immediate family.

If arriving late, are there times when a guest should *not* enter the ceremony?

Do not enter during prayers, the sermon or the eulogy. Follow ushers' guidance about entering the service.

Will the bereaved family be present at the church or funeral home before the ceremony?

Not usually, though sometimes family members do greet guests beforehand.

Is there a traditional greeting for the family?

No. Just offer your condolences.

Will there be an open casket?

Rarely. This depends on local customs and the preference of the family. "Viewing" time is sometimes scheduled in the days or hours before the funeral. "Viewing" may also be offered during or at the end of the funeral service itself.

Is a guest expected to view the body?

This is entirely optional. If there is a "viewing" at the funeral and you do not wish to participate, excuse yourself from the line that forms to pass the casket. If you happen to be in the line that passes the casket and you do not wish to view the body, simply avert your eyes.

What is appropriate behavior upon viewing the body?

View it silently and somberly. Do not touch it or place any flowers or memorabilia in the casket.

Who are the major officiants at the ceremony and what do they do?

- *A minister or pastor*, who officiates and delivers the sermon.
- Possibly a family member or a close friend, who may also deliver a eulogy.

What books are used?

The minister will use a Bible. Of several Protestant Bibles, the most commonly used in the United Church of Christ is The Holy Bible, New Revised Standard Version (New York: National Council of Churches, 1989). Also used is *The New Century Hymnal* (Cleveland, Ohio: The Pilgrim Press, 1995).

To indicate the order of the ceremony:
Usually a program will be distributed; sometimes the minister will make periodic announcements.

Will a guest who is not a member of the United Church of Christ be expected to do anything other than sit?
Guests are expected to join congregants when they stand during the service. It is entirely optional for them to read prayers aloud and sing with the congregation. In most United Church of Christ congregations, congregants do not kneel. In those churches where kneeling occurs, it is optional for guests to join in. Those guests who do not kneel should remain seated.

Are there any parts of the service in which a guest who is not a member of the United Church of Christ should not participate?
No.

If not disruptive to the ceremony, is it okay to:
◾ **Take pictures?** No.
◾ **Use a flash?** No.
◾ **Use a video camera?** No.
◾ **Use a tape recorder?** No.

Will contributions to the church be collected at the ceremony?
No.

THE INTERMENT

Should guests attend the interment?
Yes, unless the minister announces at the funeral service that the interment is only for the family.

Whom should one ask for directions?
The minister or funeral director.

What happens at the graveside?
Scriptures are read and the casket is placed in the ground.

Do guests who are not members of the United Church of Christ participate at the graveside ceremony?
No, they are simply present—although rarely, guests may be invited to say a few words about the deceased.

COMFORTING THE BEREAVED

Is it appropriate to visit the home of the bereaved after the funeral?

Often, there is a reception at the home of the bereaved after the funeral. If not, visiting a few days after the funeral is appropriate.

Will there be a religious service at the home of the bereaved?

No.

Will food be served?

Yes, possibly a dinner if there is a reception immediately after the interment.

How soon after the funeral will a mourner usually return to a normal work schedule?

The Church has no religious prescriptions specifying the number of days that one should formally be in mourning. Local, ethnic and cultural customs are more relevant than any particular religious tradition of the Church.

How soon after the funeral will a mourner usually return to a normal social schedule?

The Church has no religious prescriptions specifying the number of days that one should formally be in mourning. Local, ethnic and cultural customs are more relevant than any particular religious tradition of the Church.

Are there mourning customs to which a friend who is not a member of the United Church of Christ should be sensitive?

No. Local, ethnic and cultural customs are more relevant than any particular religious tradition of the Church.

Are there rituals for observing the anniversary of the death?

No. Local, ethnic and cultural customs are more relevant than any particular religious tradition of the Church.

38

Wesleyan

HISTORY AND BELIEFS

The Wesleyan movement, which began in the early 18th century, centers around the scriptural truth concerning the doctrine and experience of holiness, which declares that the atonement of Christ for the sins of humanity provides not only for the regeneration of sinners, but also for the entire sanctification of believers. "Regeneration" is often referred to as "The New Birth." Members of the Wesleyan Church believe that when a person repents of his or her sin and believes in Jesus Christ, then that person is also adopted into the family of God and assured of his or her salvation through the witness of the Holy Spirit. "Sanctification" is considered to be the work of the Holy Spirit through which one is separated from sin and is enabled to love God. John Wesley, whose preaching began the faith in England, referred to this teaching and experience as "perfect love."

Wesley, an Anglican priest, was a prodigious evangelical preacher, writer and organizer. While a student at Oxford University, he and his brother, Charles, led the Holy Club of devout students, whom scoffers called the "Methodists."

Wesley's teachings affirmed the freedom of human will as promoted by grace. He saw each person's depth of sin matched by the height of sanctification to which the Holy Spirit, the empowering spirit of God, can lead persons of faith.

Although Wesley remained an Anglican and disavowed attempts to form a new church, the "societies" he founded eventually became another church body known as Methodism. During a conference in Baltimore, Maryland, in 1784, the Methodist Episcopal Church was founded as an ecclesiastical organization.

John Wesley, as well as the early Methodist leaders in the United States, had uncompromisingly denounced slavery. But many ministers and members of the Methodist Episcopal Church eventually owned slaves because of the economic advantages of doing so. When some Methodist ministers in the North began to agitate for abolition, others tried to silence them. By 1843, enough churches had withdrawn from the Church to form their own denomination, which they called the Wesleyan Methodist Connection. After the Civil War, some churches in the Connection rejoined the larger Methodist body. Others were convinced that the effects of slavery had not yet been eradicated and that their stand against liquor and secret societies could best be maintained by being independent.

The church's name changed three times: In 1891, to the Wesleyan Methodist Connection (or Church) of America; in 1947, to the Wesleyan Methodist Church of America; and in 1968, to the Wesleyan Church when it merged with the Pilgrim Holiness Church. The Wesleyan Church of Canada, which consists of the Atlantic and Central districts, is the Canadian portion of the Wesleyan Church. The roots of the Central district extend back to 1889 and the former Wesleyan Methodist Church of America, while those of the Atlantic district reach back to 1888 and the Reformed Baptist Church.

Building on its abolitionist heritage, the Wesleyan Church takes strong social stands. These include opposing discrimination against interracial marriage or against age discrimination. The Church also invokes biblical principles against homosexuality and abortion, and lends moral support to any member who claims exemption from military combat as a conscientious objector and asks to service the nation as a noncombatant.

Each local church membership convenes in a local church conference at least once a year to address the business of the local church to elect the local board of administration that is chaired by the senior pastor. Members vote for the pastor of their choice and renew this at a vote taken at intervals of approximately every four years. The pastoral contract is subject to a ratifying vote by the district conference to which the local church belongs.

A quadrennial General Conference elects three General Superintendents who serve as the Church's titular, administrative and spiritual leaders. The General Conference, which is composed of equal numbers of laypersons and clergy, also elects five ministry directors and a General Secretary who serve the denomination on a full-time basis.

U.S. churches: 1,580
U.S. membership: 118,021
(*data from the* 1998 Yearbook of American and Canadian Churches)

Canadian churches: 87
Canadian membership: 7,500
(data from the Wesleyan Church of Canada, Central District)

FUNERALS AND MOURNING

The Wesleyan Church teaches that, upon the second resurrection of Christ, the just will be resurrected to eternal life. At a later date, the wicked will be resurrected into eternal damnation. (The Church maintains that a distinction in time for these two resurrections is indicated by Jesus in Luke 20:35, 36 and by St. John in Revelation 20:5, 6.) The body of the resurrected body will be whole and identifiable.

The funeral ceremony is a ceremony in itself and may last about 30 to 60 minutes.

BEFORE THE CEREMONY

How soon after the death does the funeral usually take place?

Two to three days.

What should someone who is not a member of the Wesleyan Church do upon hearing of the death of a member of that faith?

Telephone or visit the bereaved to express your condolences.

APPROPRIATE ATTIRE

Men: A jacket and tie. More casual attire is also appropriate if modest. No headcovering is required.

Women: A dress or a skirt and blouse or a pants suit. More casual attire is also appropriate if modest. Hems need not reach below the knees nor must clothing cover the arms. Open-toed shoes and modest jewelry are permissible. No headcovering is required.

Somber colors are recommended for clothing.

GIFTS

Is it appropriate to send flowers or make a contribution?

Flowers may be sent to the home of the bereaved before or after the funeral or to the funeral itself. In lieu of flowers, contributions may be made to a fund or charity designated by the family or the deceased.

Is it appropriate to send food?

Yes. This may be sent to the home of the bereaved upon hearing of the death or after the funeral.

THE CEREMONY

Where will the ceremony take place?

In a church or a funeral home or at the site of the grave itself.

When should guests arrive and where should they sit?

Arrive early. Ushers will advise guests where to sit.

If arriving late, are there times when a guest should *not* enter the ceremony?

No.

Will the bereaved family be present at the funeral site before the ceremony?

No.

Is there a traditional greeting for the family?

Just express your sympathy for the bereaved and your appreciation for the deceased.

Will there be an open casket?

Usually.

Is a guest expected to view the body?

Yes.

What is appropriate behavior upon viewing the body?

Be quiet and respectful. Gaze silently at the deceased for a brief moment.

Who are the major officiants at the ceremony and what do they do?

- *The minister,* who delivers a sermon and meditation and commits the body to the grave.
- *Musicians,* who provide music at the beginning and end of the funeral ceremony.

What books are used?

A variety of translations of the Bible are used. The most common are the New International Version and the New King James Bible.

To indicate the order of the ceremony:

The minister may make periodic announcements.

Will a guest who is not a member of the Wesleyan Church be expected to do anything other than sit?

No.

Are there any parts of the ceremony in which a guest who is not a member of the Wesleyan Church should *not* participate?

No.

If not disruptive to the ceremony, is it okay to:

◪ **Take pictures?** No.
◪ **Use a flash?** No.
◪ **Use a video camera?** No.
◪ **Use a tape recorder?** Yes.

Will contributions to the church be collected at the ceremony?

No.

THE INTERMENT

Should guests attend the interment?

This is entirely optional.

Whom should one ask for directions?

The funeral director or another member of the staff of the funeral home.

What happens at the graveside?

There is a Scripture reading, prayers are recited and the body is committed to the ground. Hymns may be sung.

Do guests who are not members of the Wesleyan Church participate at the graveside ceremony?

No. They are simply present.

COMFORTING THE BEREAVED

Is it appropriate to visit the home of the bereaved after the funeral?

Yes. The length of the visit depends on one's relationship with the bereaved and with the deceased. When visiting, express your sympathy to the bereaved and offer specific help to them. You may possibly offer a brief prayer for the deceased and reflect upon the life of the deceased.

Will there be a religious service at the home of the bereaved?

No.

Will food be served?

No.

How soon after the funeral will a mourner usually return to a normal work schedule?

Within one to two weeks.

How soon after the funeral will a mourner usually return to a normal social schedule?

Within four to five weeks.

Are there mourning customs to which a friend who is not a member of the Wesleyan Church should be sensitive?

No.

Are there rituals for observing the anniversary of the death?

No.

About SKYLIGHT PATHS Publishing

SkyLight Paths Publishing is creating a place where people of different spiritual traditions come together for challenge and inspiration, a place where we can help each other understand the mystery that lies at the heart of our existence.

Through spirituality, our religious beliefs are increasingly becoming a part of our lives—rather than apart from our lives. While many of us may be more interested than ever in spiritual growth, we may be less firmly planted in traditional religion. Yet, we do want to deepen our relationship to the sacred, to learn from our own as well as from other faith traditions, and to practice in new ways.

SkyLight Paths sees both believers and seekers as a community that increasingly transcends traditional boundaries of religion and denomination. Many people want to learn from each other, *walking together, finding the way.*

We at SkyLight Paths take great care to produce beautiful books that present meaningful spiritual content in a form that reflects the art of making high quality books. Therefore, we want to acknowledge those who contributed to the production of this book.

PRODUCTION
Marian B. Wallace & Bridgett Taylor

EDITORIAL
David O'Neal, Amanda Dupuis, Emily Wichland,
Martha McKinney & Sandra Korinchak

COVER DESIGN & TYPESETTING
Drena Fagen, New York, New York

TEXT DESIGN
Chelsea Cloeter, Chelsea Designs, Scotia, New York

TYPESETTING
Douglas S. Porter, Desktop Services & Publishing, San Antonio, Texas

COVER & TEXT PRINTING AND BINDING
Versa Press, East Peoria, Illinois

Spirituality

Honey from the Rock
An Introduction to Jewish Mysticism
by *Lawrence Kushner*

An insightful and absorbing introduction to the ten gates of Jewish mysticism and how it applies to daily life. "The easiest introduction to Jewish mysticism you can read."
6 x 9, 176 pp, Quality PB, ISBN 1-58023-073-3 **$15.95**

Eyes Remade for Wonder
The Way of Jewish Mysticism and Sacred Living
A Lawrence Kushner Reader

Intro. by *Thomas Moore*, author of *Care of the Soul*

Whether you are new to Kushner or a devoted fan, you'll find inspiration here. With samplings from each of Kushner's works, and a generous amount of new material, this book is to be read and reread, each time discovering deeper layers of meaning in our lives.
6 x 9, 240 pp, Quality PB, ISBN 1-58023-042-3 **$16.95**; HC, ISBN 1-58023-014-8 **$23.95**

Invisible Lines of Connection
Sacred Stories of the Ordinary
by *Lawrence Kushner* **AWARD WINNER!**

Through his everyday encounters with family, friends, colleagues and strangers, Kushner takes us deeply into our lives, finding flashes of spiritual insight in the process.
5½ x 8½, 160 pp, Quality PB, ISBN 1-879045-98-2 **$15.95**; HC, ISBN 1-879045-52-4 **$21.95**

Finding Joy
A Practical Spiritual Guide to Happiness
by *Dannel I. Schwartz* with *Mark Hass* **AWARD WINNER!**

Explains how to find joy through a time honored, creative—and surprisingly practical—approach based on the teachings of Jewish mysticism and Kabbalah.
6 x 9, 192 pp, Quality PB, ISBN 1-58023-009-1 **$14.95**; HC, ISBN 1-879045-53-2 **$19.95**

Ancient Secrets
Using the Stories of the Bible to Improve Our Everyday Lives
by *Rabbi Levi Meier, Ph.D.*

Drawing on a broad range of wisdom writings, distinguished rabbi and psychologist Levi Meier takes a thoughtful, wise and fresh approach to showing us how to apply the stories of the Bible to our everyday lives.
5½ x 8½, 288 pp, Quality PB, ISBN 1-58023-064-4 **$16.95**

Spirituality

Who Is My God?
An Innovative Guide to Finding Your Spiritual Identity
Created by *the Editors at SkyLight Paths*

Spiritual Type™ + Tradition Indicator = Spiritual Identity

Your Spiritual Identity is an undeniable part of who you are—whether you've thought much about it or not. This dynamic resource provides a helpful framework to begin or deepen your spiritual growth. Start by taking the unique Spiritual Identity Self-Test™; tabulate your results; then explore one, two or more of twenty-eight faiths/spiritual paths followed in America today. "An innovative and entertaining way to think—and rethink—about your own spiritual path, or perhaps even to find one." —Dan Wakefield, author of *How Do We Know When It's God?* 6 x 9, 160 pp, Quality PB Original, ISBN 1-893361-08-X **$15.95**

Spiritual Manifestos: *Visions for Renewed Religious Life in America from Young Spiritual Leaders of Many Faiths*
Edited by *Niles Elliot Goldstein*; Preface by *Martin E. Marty*

Discover the reasons why so many people have kept organized religion at arm's length.

Here, ten young spiritual leaders, most in their mid-thirties, who span the spectrum of religious traditions—Protestant, Catholic, Jewish, Buddhist, Unitarian Universalist—present the innovative ways they are transforming our spiritual communities and our lives. "These ten articulate young spiritual leaders engender hope for the vitality of 21st-century religion." —Forrest Church, Minister of All Souls Church in New York City
6 x 9, 256 pp, HC, ISBN 1-893361-09-8 **$21.95**

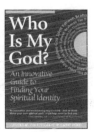
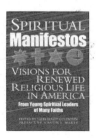
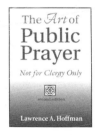

The Art of Public Prayer: *Not for Clergy Only*
by *Lawrence A. Hoffman*

A resource for worshipers today looking to change hardened worship patterns that stand in the way of everyday spirituality.

Written for laypeople and clergy of any denomination, this ecumenical introduction to meaningful public prayer is for everyone who cares about religion today.
6 x 9, 288 pp, Quality PB, ISBN 1-893361-06-3 **$17.95**

Spirituality

A Heart of Stillness
A Complete Guide to Learning the Art of Meditation
by *David A. Cooper*

The only complete, nonsectarian guide to meditation, from one of our most respected spiritual teachers.

Experience what mystics have experienced for thousands of years. *A Heart of Stillness* helps you acquire on your own, with minimal guidance, the skills of various styles of meditation. Draws upon the wisdom teachings of Christianity, Judaism, Buddhism, Hinduism, and Islam as it teaches you the processes of purification, concentration, and mastery in detail.
5½ x 8½, 272 pp, Quality PB, ISBN 1-893361-03-9 **$16.95**

Silence, Simplicity & Solitude
A Complete Guide to Spiritual Retreat at Home
by *David A. Cooper*

The classic personal spiritual retreat guide that enables readers to create their own self-guided spiritual retreat at home.

Award-winning author David Cooper traces personal mystical retreat in all of the world's major traditions, describing the varieties of spiritual practices for modern spiritual seekers. Cooper shares the techniques and practices that encompass the personal spiritual retreat experience, allowing readers to enhance their meditation practices and create an effective, self-guided spiritual retreat in their own homes—without the instruction of a meditation teacher. 5½ x 8½, 336 pp, Quality PB, ISBN 1-893361-04-7 **$16.95**

  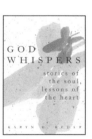  

God Whispers: *Stories of the Soul, Lessons of the Heart*
by Rabbi Karyn D. Kedar 6 x 9, 176 pp, Quality PB, ISBN 1-58023-088-1 **$15.95**;
HC, ISBN 1-58023-023-7 **$19.95**

The Empty Chair: *Finding Hope and Joy—*
Timeless Wisdom from a Hasidic Master, Rebbe Nachman of Breslov AWARD WINNER!
Adapted by Moshe Mykoff and the Breslov Research Institute
4 x 6, 128 pp, Deluxe PB, 2-color text, ISBN 1-879045-67-2 **$9.95**

The Gentle Weapon: *Prayers for Everyday and Not-So-Everyday Moments*
Adapted from the Wisdom of Rebbe Nachman of Breslov by Moshe Mykoff and
S. C. Mizrahi, with the Breslov Research Institute
4 x 6, 144 pp, Deluxe PB, 2-color text, ISBN 1-58023-022-9 **$9.95**

Children's Spirituality

God Said Amen

by *Sandy Eisenberg Sasso*

Full-color illus. by *Avi Katz*

For ages 4 & up

MULTICULTURAL, NONDENOMINATIONAL, NONSECTARIAN

A warm and inspiring tale of two kingdoms: Midnight Kingdom is overflowing with water but has no oil to light its lamps; Desert Kingdom is blessed with oil but has no water to grow its gardens. The kingdoms' rulers ask God for help but are too stubborn to ask each other. It takes a minstrel, a pair of royal riding-birds and their young keepers, and a simple act of kindness to show that they need only reach out to each other to find the answers to their prayers.

9 x 12, 32 pp, HC, Full-color illus., ISBN 1-58023-080-6 **$16.95**

For Heaven's Sake

For ages 4 & up

by *Sandy Eisenberg Sasso*; Full-color illus. by *Kathryn Kunz Finney*

Everyone talked about heaven: "Thank heavens." "Heaven forbid." "For heaven's sake, Isaiah." But no one would say what heaven was or how to find it. So Isaiah decides to find out, by seeking answers from many different people. "This book is a reminder of how well Sandy Sasso knows the minds of children. But it may surprise—and delight—readers to find how well she knows us grown-ups too." —*Maria Harris*, National Consultant in Religious Education, and author of *Teaching and Religious Imagination*

9 x 12, 32 pp, HC, Full-color illus., ISBN 1-58023-054-7 **$16.95**

But God Remembered:

Stories of Women from Creation to the Promised Land

For ages 8 & up

by *Sandy Eisenberg Sasso*; Full-color illus. by *Bethanne Andersen*

A fascinating collection of four different stories of women only briefly mentioned in biblical tradition and religious texts. Award-winning author Sasso vibrantly brings to life courageous and strong women from ancient tradition; all teach important values through their actions and faith. "Exquisite. . . . A book of beauty, strength and spirituality." —*Association of Bible Teachers* 9 x 12, 32 pp, HC, Full-color illus., ISBN 1-879045-43-5 **$16.95**

God in Between

For ages 4 & up

by *Sandy Eisenberg Sasso*; Full-color illus. by *Sally Sweetland*

If you wanted to find God, where would you look? A magical, mythical tale that teaches that God can be found where we are: within all of us and the relationships between us. "This happy and wondrous book takes our children on a sweet and holy journey into God's presence." —*Rabbi Wayne Dosick, Ph.D.*, author of *Golden Rules* and *Soul Judaism*

9 x 12, 32 pp, HC, Full-color illus., ISBN 1-879045-86-9 **$16.95**

Children's Spirituality

In Our Image
God's First Creatures

For ages 4 & up

by *Nancy Sohn Swartz*
Full-color illus. by *Melanie Hall*

A playful new twist on the Creation story—from the perspective of the animals. Celebrates the interconnectedness of nature and the harmony of all living things. "The vibrantly colored illustrations nearly leap off the page in this delightful interpretation." —School Library Journal

"A message all children should hear, presented in words and pictures that children will find irresistible." —*Rabbi Harold Kushner*, author of *When Bad Things Happen to Good People*

9 x 12, 32 pp, HC, Full-color illus., ISBN 1-879045-99-0 **$16.95**

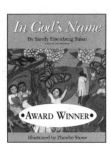

God's Paintbrush

For ages 4 & up

by *Sandy Eisenberg Sasso*; Full-color illus. by *Annette Compton*

Invites children of all faiths and backgrounds to encounter God openly in their own lives. Wonderfully interactive; provides questions adult and child can explore together at the end of each episode. "An excellent way to honor the imaginative breadth and depth of the spiritual life of the young." —*Dr. Robert Coles*, Harvard University
11 x 8½, 32 pp, HC, Full-color illus., ISBN 1-879045-22-2 **$16.95**

Also available: **A Teacher's Guide**
8½ x 11, 32 pp, PB, ISBN 1-879045-57-5 **$6.95**

God's Paintbrush Celebration Kit 9½ x 12, HC, Includes 5 sessions/40 full-color Activity Sheets and Teacher Folder with complete instructions, ISBN 1-58023-050-4 **$21.95**

In God's Name

For ages 4 & up

by *Sandy Eisenberg Sasso*; Full-color illus. by *Phoebe Stone*

Like an ancient myth in its poetic text and vibrant illustrations, this award-winning modern fable about the search for God's name celebrates the diversity and, at the same time, the unity of all the people of the world. "What a lovely, healing book!" —*Madeleine L'Engle*
9 x 12, 32 pp, HC, Full-color illus., ISBN 1-879045-26-5 **$16.95**

Children's Spirituality

Becoming Me: *A Story of Creation*
by *Martin Boroson*
Full-color illus. by *Christopher Gilvan-Cartwright*

For ages 4 & up

NONDENOMINATIONAL, NONSECTARIAN

Told in the personal "voice" of the Creator, here is a story about creation and relationship that is about each one of us. In simple words and with radiant illustrations, the Creator tells an intimate story about love, about friendship and playing, about our world—and about ourselves. And with each turn of the page, we're reminded that we just might be closer to our Creator than we think!

8 x 10, 32 pp, Full-color illus., HC, ISBN 1-893361-11-X **$16.95**

A Prayer for the Earth
The Story of Naamah, Noah's Wife
by *Sandy Eisenberg Sasso*
Full-color illus. by *Bethanne Andersen*

For ages 4 & up

NONDENOMINATIONAL, NONSECTARIAN

This new story, based on an ancient text, opens readers' religious imaginations to new ideas about the well-known story of the Flood. When God tells Noah to bring the animals of the world onto the ark, God also calls on Naamah, Noah's wife, to save each plant on Earth. "A lovely tale. . . . Children of all ages should be drawn to this parable for our times." —*Tomie de Paola*, artist/author of books for children
9 x 12, 32 pp, HC, Full-color illus., ISBN 1-879045-60-5 **$16.95**

The 11th Commandment
Wisdom from Our Children
by The Children of America

For all ages

MULTICULTURAL, NONDENOMINATIONAL, NONSECTARIAN

"If there were an Eleventh Commandment, what would it be?" Children of many religious denominations across America answer this question—in their own drawings and words. "A rare book of spiritual celebration for all people, of all ages, for all time."—Bookviews
8 x 10, 48 pp. HC, Full-color illus., ISBN 1-879045-46-X **$16.95**

What Is God's Name? (A Board Book)
An abridged board book version of the award-winning *In God's Name.*

For ages 0–4

5 x 5, 24 pp, Board, Full-color illus., ISBN 1-893361-10-1 **$7.95**

  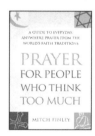